Heaven's Perspective

By Leslie Lott

Retold by Leslie Lott McAlpin

Preface

Over 2500 years ago, Lao Tzu wrote the *Tao Te Ching*. It is considered one of the great works of spiritual enlightenment. In these wise poems, Lao Tzu expresses beautiful, eternal truths including his knowing that we are all one.

At the very outset, however, he makes note of the limitations of language. He writes: The Tao that can be told is not the universal Tao. The name that can be named is not the universal name.

Lao Tzu knew that what he aimed to describe was indescribable in human terms.

It is largely due to just such limitations of language that I was hesitant to write this story earlier.

Yet those limitations did not keep Lao Tzu from writing. In the end, despite his awareness of the limitations, Lao Tzu chose to write of what he knew. Clearly he must have felt that for him to write of another dimension—even via the limited language available to him in this dimension-- would be better than to not write of the eternal truths at all.

Though I know full well that the very act of putting my story into words will necessarily diminish it, I have nonetheless also chosen to write of what I now know. As best I am able, I will give you heaven's perspective via a language of earth.

I take my cue from Lao Tzu.

Allons! To that which is endless, as it was beginningless.

--Walt Whitman

Excerpted from Song of the Open Road

Chapter 1

Einstein, Helicopters, and Heaven's Perspective

The year 2005 was a big year for me. I died, went to heaven, and came back to earth.

Actually, that's not entirely accurate. Although my body died, the part of me that is most essentially "me" stayed very much alive. That's the part of me that went to heaven.

Of course, my body stayed here on earth. When I left heaven, I came back to the physical part of me (my body) and resumed life here.

But NOTHING has been the same since I got back. Not a single thing.

How can life on earth possibly be the same after you have been in heaven and have memory and knowledge of that realm? It cannot be the same. Not at all.

It's a life changer...in every possible way.

Heaven is certainly not an easy place to leave, but ultimately it was my decision to come back here. I was shown some things I still wanted to do on earth, and I came back to do them.

This is the story of my journey to heaven and back: how it happened, what I experienced, why I returned to earth, and the joyful knowing that I now have about all the questions our souls want to understand.

What happens when we die?

Will I miss my body?

What is heaven like?

What is the meaning of life?

Why is life sometimes so hard?

Why do some people get sick or have accidents and die "before their time" while others don't?

Why is there so much sadness on earth?

Why is life sometimes so hard?

Why do some people seem to have more challenges than others?

How can I enjoy life to the fullest?

While in heaven, the answer to each of the above questions (and many others!) was known to me the moment I formed each query. Having the opportunity to live on earth with *heaven's perspective* is spectacular. It has allowed me to live on earth in a completely different way.

Einstein said (roughly paraphrasing) that it is impossible to solve a problem from the level at which it was created. I've thought quite a bit about what he meant by that. The following analogy makes it clear why what Einstein said on this issue is so valuable when we're in a rough place in our lives.

The analogy is what I call *The Helicopter Story*. It goes like this:

Imagine you are driving on a highway that is busy. You are on a trip in a new city, and you have never been on this stretch of road before in your life but you have directions and know where you are going. (In case you are wondering, you are in a rental car that does not have a GPS and your cell phone is out of commission.)

Although there is lots of traffic on the road with you, traffic is generally flowing smoothly until you go around a bend in the road and find that in front of you the traffic is slowing down so much that you need to tap the brakes. You look further up ahead and note that as far as you are able to see, traffic is backed up.

As you move forward, now by inches rather than miles, you only seem to get deeper into the congestion until traffic slows to a complete halt, and there you are: stuck. There is definitely some kind of a problem up ahead, but you can't see what the actual problem is.

You can't see the problem because you are at the same level that the problem originated on. You are on the road—and so is the problem. This means that you do not know if the issue ahead is construction, if there might have been an accident, or if perhaps the road is gridlocked for some other reason.

Let's say you make the assumption that there was likely an accident of some type since you don't see any signs of construction. Even so, you certainly cannot know how many vehicles were involved and whether the road is completely blocked or not. You have no idea if it's best to take the exit just ahead, or if taking that nearby exit would be even worse. It seems everyone is trying to get to that exit, and now the exit ramp is completely bottlenecked, too. You have no information to help you make a decision about what to do because you are on the level of the problem--on the road, in the traffic jam itself.

By chance, you spot a helicopter flying high above the road. You know that the pilot, just an ordinary person, is able to see things that you cannot since the pilot is above the problem and you are IN the problem. You wonder... What does that helicopter pilot see?

From his/her perch above the highway, the pilot sees that the accident involved a semi-truck. The truck appears to be the only vehicle that was in the accident, but the truck's trailer is now blocking five of the six lanes of the highway. No emergency vehicles are on the scene yet. The helicopter pilot also sees routes leading away from the congested highway. Some are clear. Others are also backed up. The pilot sees all of this and more... but you don't have access to what the pilot sees.

But then, the helicopter swoops in just close enough for you to be able to barely make out something on the side of the helicopter. It says... what? Ah!! They are NUMBERS. This must be a helicopter from local news radio station! Perfect!! You turn on the car radio and quickly punch in the numbers you saw on the side of the helicopter. You get there in time to catch the following:

....and so, if you are heading northbound anywhere between mile markers 60 and 78, we urge you to get off the highway and take an alternate route. From up here we see some heavy congestion on some of the alternate routes but others are fine. The least congested routes are via exit 62 and exit 74, and we suggest you exit on those to avoid additional delays because those routes are clear just beyond the exits themselves. The other exits are a mess long after the exit ramp, so avoid those. **But definitely get off that highway!**

There's no telling how long it will be before a tow truck can make it through the miles of traffic now backed up --and with that black liquid we mentioned earlier continuing to ooze from the truck, there could be some kind of additional problem as well....

You turn off the radio and give thanks for that helicopter and its bird's-eye view of the situation. As luck would have it, the exit you are sitting next to is 62. It seems pretty congested, and you most likely wouldn't have taken this exit if you hadn't just gotten that news from the helicopter, but now that you have heard what the pilot sees —and you know the pilot can see much more than you can from your spot stuck in traffic on the road-- you go ahead and get into the exit lane for exit 62 and... TA-DUM! Within just a few minutes you are completely out of the congestion and back to moving at a normal speed once again.

It might almost have seemed like getting that information was magic if you didn't know about the existence of helicopters. However, since you *do* know helicopters exist, and you also understand the nature of the higher perspective, it seems totally normal to you that the helicopter pilot just gave you information to solve your problem, and that's why you exited and are now sailing along.

You continue on your way while wondering about all of those folks who didn't hear the helicopter pilot's perspective. They are still stuck in the problem. But you, by gaining access to a higher perspective, were able to solve the problem... just as Einstein knew to be the case.

And, that, my friends, is my Helicopter Story. As you can see from the story, perspective is the key. From a higher place, we can see a problem without being embroiled in it, and from that higher place we are also able to see the situation/problem in its entirety. From that higher place, we see more and so we see more options and more information, and (therefore) we can easily select the best path to take.

With the helicopter story, you didn't need to leave the road yourself. You only needed to get the perspective of the person above the road. That is the concept behind this book.

What I'd like to do in the pages ahead is give those who are open to it a new perspective of life on earth from the perspective of the place I went when I left my body. In other words, I'd like to share Heaven's Perspective with you.

Why? Because as I look around at life on earth, while I see a lot happening that is magnificent, I also see many people struggling and trying to solve their struggles from the level of earth—from the level at which the problem (whatever it may be) exists. If we take what Einstein said and really consider it, we recognize that it is logical that getting a perspective from a higher level could be extremely useful in solving our problems (from the personal to the global) here on earth.

Just as the pilot in our helicopter example is a normal person who happens to be in a helicopter, I am a regular person who happened to leave earth, go to heaven, and come back to earth. Because of this, I have a window on the way that life is seen from heaven, and it is completely different from the way most of us see life while we are on earth.

By reading about the perspective I gained while in heaven, you will have an opportunity to see things differently: to see life in the way it is seen/known/experienced in heaven.

With the perspective of heaven, you will have achieved what Einstein said is necessary for solving problems (whatever your earthly problem or problems may be), and from that place you will see clearly how best to move forward.

If you choose, in addition to learning about what I saw, you can use the things I learned to actually go up to a higher place yourself. You will have the option to become lighter. Think of a balloon filled with helium. Up it goes!! Lighter things rise. So do lighter people.

It is my intention that this material be used by all who read it to create joy in all aspects of their lives here on earth-- if that is their desire. The tools for living your life to the fullest are waiting lovingly for you in the pages that follow.

My invitation to you: Read and ascend if you so choose.

If you are still with me and are reading these words, get comfortable and settle in for a wonderful story. And, by the way, this story is far better than any fairy tale you have ever heard. Why? Because not only is this story magical...it is also 100% real.

Chapter 2

How It Happened

I remember lying down on the table before my operation. It stands out because it was a moment I had planned and looked forward to for a very long time, yet when it finally arrived I found myself feeling uncomfortable. I was physically cold in the gown I had been given, plus I felt very exposed and vulnerable. For the first time it dawned on me that people I didn't know well (or at all) were going to be looking at my naked body.

YIKES! What if I have a kooky stray hair in some freaky place and they all laugh at me???

Calm down. I quickly told myself. Just breathe, Leslie. Relax. You're prepared for this. It's going to be fine.

There would be no wimping out at this point. I had come too far for that. My life after the operation was going to be a new life. I would have normal breasts for a woman of my height and weight. I'd be proportionate and feel physically like the woman I was in all other ways. I'd be able to wear a dress that fit without having to get it altered to make the top smaller. I'd be able to wear a bathing suit without feeling completely embarrassed. But more than any of that, I was going to finally feel comfortable in my body.

Yes. I'm ready for this. A new era of my life is ahead of me.

After all, I was finally doing what I'd wanted to do for at least five years. For months after deciding I'd really do it, I'd meticulously researched the best doctors in the field as well as the best type, size, shape, and placement of breast implants taking into consideration my own height, weight, age, current breast tissue, and every other possible detail. Based on (even more) research, I had made the decision to have my implants inserted through the armpits and to have them placed under the breast muscle so they would look more natural even though I knew the recovery time would be longer that way. I knew what was coming and was ready.

Or so I thought!

No matter how well I'd prepared, I could not have planned for what was about to happen.

A very nice woman said something to calm me, and then things went fuzzy and I faded out.

The next thing I remember clearly is that I was hovering up near the ceiling looking down on what appeared to be some sort of operating room. I was up near a corner and I saw some people below me near the one bed/table in the room. They were focused on the table and the person lying on it.

It seemed perfectly normal and natural that I was floating up near the ceiling of this room watching this scene. The form I was in felt like pure energy, and it seemed like I had always been in this form. I never thought to wonder where I'd been before popping into position near the ceiling. I simply WAS. And, I was thinking of myself as Leslie, just as always. It was known to me/by me that I was Leslie and I was "whole" in the form that I was in. It seemed normal that I was consciousness with no physical aspect.

I therefore had no grasp of the fact that I had been in a physical form until just a moment ago, and I certainly didn't remember that I'd been inside the very body that was on that table below.

In fact, the scene below seemed unrelated to me in any way apart from the coincidence that I happened to be observing it. The connection between me and the body below was not a part of my consciousness. For the first moment of my awareness of myself as a floating individual in a room with something happening below me, I just neutrally watched the situation under me. My attention was focused on the table and the people near it.

The scene below was in my line of vision, but it wasn't something I was overly curious about learning more about. It just happened to be where my attention was focused when I became aware of being in that hovering location, so I watched it casually -- the way you might watch a moment or two of a TV show you happen upon when clicking through channels. In that way it was similar to watching something on television. It was also similar to a TV show in that I was able to see it and it was there below and before me, but I knew the events were occurring in a different dimension from where I was-- much like the way we know the people on a TV screen are *not* in our home even though they *are* in our home.

And so, these people down in the room were in the same room I was in... but at the same time they were not where I was. They were like TV-people: they were there but NOT there. This wasn't TV though, and I knew that.

Just as when watching TV you know what you are watching is happening in the 'land of TV', I was aware that what I was watching was happening in a realm where people were in bodies and did not float as I did. The beings were in physical bodies and were following laws of physics for bodies in physical form. I was not in physical form and was not in a dimension of things physical nor was I following the laws of physics. I was not a physical being, and *that* felt completely normal. Observing this other dimension – the physical dimension before me -- peacefully and with mild curiosity also seemed normal.

But as I watched the activity another moment, I was pulled into the situation the way we can get pulled into a TV show. And that was when I actually looked at the body on the table for the first time.

HUH! I feel a connection to that body. What is that about?

Wait.... Hang on....That is **my** body.

No. That WAS my body. I don't have a body now.

As I really looked at the body, there was a kind of jolt of recognition. I now knew there was a connection between the *hovering Leslie* in the non-physical dimension of that room and the *body that had been Leslie* which was in the physical dimension of that same room.

I was in the room because that was my body down there. At the same time that I understood the connection, there was also a complete and neutral understanding of the fact that my body, or my *former* body, was dead.

How odd. That body looks frail, but apart from that it looks like a completely normal body.

For the first time, I was able to see my body as others had seen my body, and it looked entirely different than I had imagined it looked when I had been inside it. I had always viewed myself as unattractive and overweight. From outside of the body, however, it was clear that this body's face was not ugly at all. It was just a normal face. This body was not overweight at all either. In fact, it seemed to be pretty average. How odd that I had had so much drama about things that didn't exist outside my own mind.

Huh. Interesting.

I noted all of these things in the instant I recognized the body.

Yet I remained completely detached emotionally with no feelings of loss or sadness about the end of my life on earth. I did not feel any desire to return to the dimension of physical existence.

People since have asked me if I tried to connect with or contact anyone in the room below me. I did not. There seemed no reason to. I had no desire to make contact with the physical world.

I felt nothing more than mild interest that my body was dead as I watched the people below attempting to revive me. It didn't really seem to matter much that the body was dead since I was so very much alive. The feeling of neutrality about it all was most prominent feeling. That, and the feeling of peace.

Life on earth suddenly seemed like a very small part of something much bigger. Although I was dead to the people in the dimension I was looking at, I also understood that I, Leslie --the me I have always been and continued to be beyond the death of my body-- was completely alive.

All of these things happened in a very short period of time. It was only moments after finding myself hovering in the room that I realized the body on the table below was my body. With the awareness that I was dead but still alive, I was suddenly gone from that room ... and in a place very, very different.

Chapter 3

The Particles

Years ago there was a commercial for some sort of over-the-counter capsule. When I think back to my age at the time the commercial was airing, I think the commercial was probably on TV at some point in the 70s. Considering the focus of the ad, it was probably around the time they were just discovering ways to deliver over the counter medicine in doses other than the traditional pill or liquid formats. In this particular commercial, the idea was to emphasize that this medicine was available in a capsule form and that the capsule had thousands of little beads of medicine inside the outer shell.

The outer shell was comprised of two pieces that could be pulled apart. Now, if the two halves of the outer shell were to be pulled apart in a non-TV, non-staged setting, the little pieces inside would follow the laws of physics and would simply drop to the surface below the capsule. They would look like the multi-colored sprinkles that are often on top of sugar cookies, and these little sprinkles of medicine would just fall to the surface-- in real life.

But this was a commercial and everything was staged to emphasize the tiny beads inside the outer shell.

This was done by first showing a close-up of the capsule against a white background. The viewer saw the hands of a person whose body was not visible. This person was holding the capsule in two hands. One end of the capsule was between one thumb and index finger and the other end of the capsule was between the person's other thumb and index finger.

The camera then zoomed in even closer and showed the capsule's details and focused on the place in the center of the capsule where the ends of the two different halves of the outer shell came together.

Then the person pulled (maybe twisted?) and the two halves of the capsule separated and the little beads which had previously been inside the capsule were released.

Only they didn't fall to the surface below the capsule. And they didn't move at anywhere near real-time speed.

The multi-colored pieces floated slowly outward (not downward!) from the place where they had been enclosed in the capsule. They were being released... being set free... and they floated outward scattering in all directions. The multiple colors scattered slowly and every single one was visible against the white background.

I was mesmerized each time this commercial reached the part where the beads slowly scattered.

It had been simulated to look as if the capsule was being opened in a space where the law of gravity was not in effect. The little beads – it looked like at least a hundred thousand of them to my child's mind– floated in all different directions when they were released from the capsule.

That's how it felt in the place I was now in.

Chapter 4

The Light

I was in a place that was filled with light.

No.

It isn't correct to describe it as filled with light.

It is more accurate to say that the place was *made* of light.

And the light was intelligent. It was... LOVE.

When I say "light" you might think of light as it is on earth.
But heavenly light is so, so, *so*, *so*, very much more.

For starters, there is more *inside* of it. Somehow it actually
contains *more*. It is as if it has more ingredients in it than the
light we experience here on earth. Light here on earth is light,
yes. But the light there is more like light PLUS.

And it's this *plus* part that I am having a hard time describing.
It is simply more-- more everything. It is more luminous and
somehow it is also more white and more beautiful and more
true than any light I have ever seen on earth. Light there is
also conscious and it can communicate and was
communicating with me.

The first time I tried to explain this initial impression to people after I came back, they thought I meant a light from a specific source was talking to me.

It was not that way at all. First, there was no talking as we know "talking" on earth to be. Language there is closer to telepathy. Second, there was no specific *form* that the light was emanating from. Rather the space WAS the light and the light *was* the space, and the messages were coming to me from all different areas within this realm of light.

There was no empty or un-light-filled space in this place. All of it was full of love/light (love in the form of light). I was floating within that light, and at the same time I maintained knowledge of myself as the separate entity, Leslie.

All of those little sprinkly particles of me (that had come out of the "capsule" of my body) were now there with all of the other particles that made up the light of all that is. My particles were floating there, grouped together in something like a small, loose cloud in the light. While I understood I was "me", I also understood that I was also a part of the larger light as well.

Since coming back to earth, the closest analogy I have found to describe this initial feeling is the eastern concept of the ocean existing as GOD/HEAVEN/ALL THAT IS. We all come from the ocean. Then a cup is dipped into the ocean and we exist in that cup (a body) rather than in the ocean, yet we are still a part of the ocean even when we are in the cup. While the cup represents the body on earth, the ocean represents where we come from and where we go after our body dies. We continue to be a part of the whole even when in the cup/a body, but it is easy to forget we are a part of the whole as long as we are in a distinct form.

Being there really was in many ways like being in an ocean of love in the form of light, but this realm was far larger than the largest ocean on earth. And while this analogy helps to explain some aspects of what I experienced in heaven, there is a big difference from this ocean analogy and heaven in that while in heaven, I always maintained a very clear awareness of myself as a separate entity. I didn't just mix back into the ocean of light and lose awareness of myself as Leslie. Somehow, in that realm, it is possible to be part of the ocean and maintain a sense of individuality as well.

In addition to the fact that this light which was everywhere was spectacularly beautiful, it was also shimmering in a way that light does not shimmer on earth. The sparkling was somewhat like the way that sunlight can glisten and bounce off water. Except here there was no water. It was only light. And the light itself was joyful with a joy beyond explanation.

It also felt to me that this very special light included all of *all that is* -- all of the things that comprise all of all we know here on earth as well as many things that we here in physical bodies cannot imagine or hold within our mind's grasp. All that exists everywhere IS light... just in different forms.

And the light was love and the love was light and they were not separable. And while on earth love exists in different amounts of dilutedness, there in heaven it is in its *undiluted* form and that form is love expressed as light.

Calling it love/light makes sense because they are one and the same there. We have no word that I can find in English for this concept. Radiant, beaming, flowing love... all of this is light. But it's not only that the light was made of love. The light was also *sending* me its love.

Unconditionally.

There were other wonderful-feeling emotions in the light as well. The fullness and depth of these emotions within the light of "all that is" are hard for me to process now that I am back in my body on earth. Sometimes, however, on a beautiful day when I see the sun streaming through the clouds in such a way that the rays seem to be more than just rays of light from the sun, my eyes fill with tears of joy as I remember being

27

there in that light/love of True Home. I will go back there someday, but right now I have things left to do here on earth.

If I were asked to summarize my initial "knowings" about the place I had suddenly found myself in, I would say: *the fabric of heaven is love and all that exists everywhere is made of this exquisite, conscious fabric.*

And in that first moment as I was floating there in what seemed to be a never-ending expanse of pure love/light, the love shone on me and into me and through me. The light was communicating with me, and I understood all that it said to me.

It was welcoming me.

Chapter 5

Welcome Messages

In the instant I found myself in this wonderful realm, I was aware of the messages pouring into me from all directions. The information coming into me was being absorbed by me instantaneously, and I both *knew* this information to be true and *felt* it to be true at the same time. In this place it seemed normal that feeling and knowing were experienced as the same thing.

So, there I was, fully myself --though with no physical body-- in the middle of a huge expanse of pure love expressing itself as light while from all directions, beautiful things were being whispered to me about me and about the nature of the realm of love and of all existence.

It felt as if the light-filled messages were almost being "blown" gently to me and when they landed on me it was as if they melted into me and kind of became a part of me. All of these messages were filled with more joy and love than I had ever felt before.

There was an air of celebration, and my joy increased as I understood that the celebration was for me and also for all existence itself... and it was clear that I was somehow both.

Although this amazing space of light seemed to be as big as the entire universe, and I was simply there, floating in it and receiving these most precious messages, nothing in any of this seemed or felt even the *least* bit unusual to me. I continued on: just happily hovering as a cluster of particles within that joyful, conscious, light-filled dimension—as if it were the most natural thing that could be happening.

These sacred "whispered" messages from the light continued and they came to me as distinct and separate messages, but they also all fit together in a coordinated manner. These light messages had no color associated with them; however, it was almost as if they *were* all different colors of light in the sense that they all felt somehow like different "aspects" of the larger light.

In the way that the light-messages were separate and also coordinated, it was similar to having each of the colors of the rainbow communicate with me separately, and the message from each variation of the light carried a slightly different version of the main theme. But because there was actually no visual distinction within the white light, this was something I sensed, not saw. These separate messages then flowed together upon greeting me--and they somehow combined. As all of the separate messages came together, they kept their individuality but also blended into a larger message of love, unity, peace, and welcome--made up of all the individual smaller messages of love.

Many of the messages I received in heaven came in this manner: reaching me like the one voice formed by a chorus of voices except that the messages were not coming from one general direction as they would if a choir was singing. Instead, they were coming to me from completely different areas within an infinitely larger whole--coming from many different directions and all blending in truth and love. I felt almost like I was in the middle of a huge arena of light filled with love for me and for all, and from all the different "seats" messages of love were being sent to me in my position-- in what felt like the center of the arena.

The way the messages blended, it also felt like beautiful musical chords with distinct sounds that combine to make more complex sounds, but this wasn't music per se. It was information/love/light/truth/joy all in one.

And these messages went into me and became a part of me as if a snowflake that melts in your hand could then somehow be absorbed by your skin --although of course I didn't have hands and there was no snow. Yet I absorbed these messages in a similar way.

While I *saw* no distinctions in the light, within the messages themselves there were different kinds of "fingerprints" so that I knew without a doubt that different essences were somehow sending them from within the whole. One "chord" was saying something like this:

Everything is love. You are a part of that everything. Love is perfect, eternal, infinite. You are perfect, eternal, infinite. All is perfect, eternal infinite. Light is love. *Love is light.* You are light. *You are love.* We love you. *We light you.*

The whispered messages landed softly on my essence, my soul, and each one made me glow with its gentleness and sincerity, its purity and unconditional love for me.

Though these messages came in at the same time, none of them were distorted or drowned out by the others so that I was able to absorb them all. In addition to the messages themselves being unconditionally loving, the immense love and joy of the senders themselves was somehow *also* IN the messages.

I saw only the breath-taking light uniformly everywhere and in all directions, but I was now certain that there were multitudes of different essences within this light/love and that they were the sending me these messages of light from the light--all via light.

Another message-chord was something like this:

Welcome home/love/perfection. Welcome home/truth/light. Welcome home/joy/freedom. Welcome home/peace/one. Welcome home/all/ALL. Welcome home/we/you. *We welcome you home/peace/love/light/joy/truth.*

These words that are listed with slashes between them came to me almost as a single concept rather than as individual words. It was as if these words that are distinct concepts in English were blended into more complex concepts there and they came to me in that more complex-concept form than I can express with an earth language.

The reason that was possible and the reason it was possible for me to process all of this is because these messages were not coming to me in words exactly. It was more as if it was the *essence* of each message that was being sent to me.

Words seem too far removed from the essence of a thing for the things I was receiving to be called actual words.

My welcome was spectacular.

I was surrounded by light that loved me, I was a part of that light, and I was in my true home.

Chapter 6

A Sense

Years ago, I went to Egypt. While there I greatly enjoyed browsing in the outdoor bazaars because of the excitement of the organized chaos. Hopeful sellers shouted out information about their wares in an international sellers' language of gestures and Arabic peppered with snippets of any other languages they thought might get someone's attention. As I explored, it was hot, it was extremely dry, and everything was dusty. With each step I took, little puffs of dust made clouds around my feet.

However, I wasn't looking at my feet much because there was so much to see everywhere around me. Each booth held new surprises. In one, there were mounds upon mounds of exotic spices overflowing from bins and baskets and bags. In another, piles of hand-woven rugs were stacked like the gigantic fabric pages of some long-forgotten manuscript. Elegant, flowing dresses with lovingly-embroidered panels hung immediately adjacent to mass produced t-shirts while in another stall, colored glass lanterns in geometric designs were suspended above intricate silver jewelry. The walls between the booths were shared in such a way that one booth led immediately to another and another and another as far as the eye could see.

In the street, animals of varying sizes wandered freely or pulled carts, and a group of boys kicked a soccer ball while dodging loose animals and irritated vendors. Birds for sale, some leashed others caged, squawked in protest near a young girl drawing in the dirt who seemed oblivious to the goings-on around her. A woman, perhaps the girl's mother, draped a variety of handmade satchels on me the instant I paused. I gestured a "no thanks" to her and then pushed ahead --going even deeper into this fantastic party for the senses. I walked and walked and walked. Zoning officers would have a melt-down here. I loved this place!

At one point I came upon a stall that had lots of itsy-bitsy glass jars filled with mysterious liquids. I was intrigued and slowed my pace to get a longer look. Each little jar appeared to have a kind of squeezable top on it and from this a hollow tube went downward into the jar in such a way that it looked as if there was an eye-dropper in each jar. What was this place selling?

A wonderfully wrinkled old man appeared out of nowhere and his eyes twinkled as if he had the world's best-kept secret here in his little shop. I smiled and he took this as encouragement to dive right into prices; pointing to jars and saying many things in Arabic that I could not understand. I *did* understand the numbers-- which were in English. This got me even more curious because whatever this was that he was selling, it was expensive.

After doing some basic exchange-rate math in my mind, I determined that each little jar cost more than I would typically spend back home on roughly two and a half weeks of groceries. I knew enough about the bizarres to know that haggling was expected, but even so... he was starting off pretty high. I wondered if the jars held some kind of medicine-- or possibly even an illegal drug? I decided it might be best to walk on, partly for that reason, but also because this was far more than I was planning to spend on all my gifts combined.

But before I could step away, the man did something that held me in my position. He began waving his hands slowly in the air in front of all the bottles while mumbling quietly to himself. It was as if he was a forgetful magician looking for his favorite potion in order to cast the perfect spell, and I was--once again-- intrigued. I looked on until his hands suddenly stopped moving in front of an almost full jar that had one red and two gold stripes on it.

He picked that bottle up so tenderly that I just *had* to see what he would do next. I stepped closer to see better and watched as he very slowly and deliberately pressed the plastic piece on top of the bottle in such a way that the minutest amount of a clear, viscous liquid moved up into the hollow tube.

I held my breath waiting to see what he would next do. I could just imagine him slowly pulling back his eyelid and carefully releasing a drop into his eye… but instead—now moving with lightening speed-- he reached over and squeezed the eyedropper over one of my hands!

With a quick "plup" it was done, and the tiniest bit of the mystery liquid was on my skin before my reflexes could kick in.

I couldn't believe it. What was this liquid?

Before I had a chance to even make a sound, an exquisite smell hit my nose and I was transported from my place of concern (and sweat and dust) to a space of utter and perfect calm. I was rooted to the spot.

The liquid --or rather the smell from the liquid-- was wafting up to my nose from that drop on my hand. And I started to laugh when I understood.

The twinkly old man?

He was selling **perfume**.

What a good salesman he was. He had me! He stood holding the bottle and smiling at me. What a smart man!! The whole show had been a sales presentation, and I was one hooked fish.

All I was thinking about now was whether the other bottles held equally amazing treasures. Maybe it was just this one bottle that was unique in its magnificence?

He gestured for me to put something under my nose and sniff in order to clear the first scent. I took the small bowl he held out for me which looked and smelled like it contained coffee beans. I inhaled and it was, indeed, coffee.

Before I could give him back the bowl, he was at it again! He now squeezed another unimaginably small drop from a *different* bottle (with three glittery green stripes on it) onto my wrist --which was exposed as I held the bowl with the scent-clearing coffee beans.

I was FLOORED!!! This scent was different than the first yet equally amazing. How could this be? What was going on here? How could I have never before experienced such pure and intense smells?

I looked at the man and he saw the questions in my face.

He said: "A Sense."

I continued to stare, not understanding.

He then went on in broken English that conveyed most of what he desired to communicate: "Pure Perfume. Not mix with water like in store. Never fade. **TRUE** thing is A sense."

When he said the word 'true', he drew it out and said it louder than the other words to emphasize his point.

Now gesturing with love toward his entire collection of bottles, he said once more: **A sense.**

And then I understood.

He was trying to say ESSENCE! This vendor had the *essences* of perfumes for sale. He was selling the pure oil that perfumes are made from. It was something I had never been around before and that was why these smells were so much more than anything I had ever encountered.

Not long before my trip to Egypt, I had taught English to a woman from Paris whose job it was to create perfumes. Because of a passing comment she had made as class had been ending one day, we had had a conversation in which she had given me the very basics about how perfumes are created. It was only because of that chance conversation that I had any clue at all what perfume essences even were…. And now here I was smelling them!

I took that as a sign. If need be, I wouldn't eat for two and a half weeks after my trip, but I was going to buy my favorite essence as a gift to myself. I stayed in that little stall a long time, and I smelled the liquid in almost every bottle.

I ended up buying that very first essence I had smelled. To this day, I still have no idea what it was/is actually the essence *of*. I do know that it was one of the best purchases I have made in my entire life. Even now, that tiny bottle with the red and gold stripes still has a little bit of essence left in it. The lid is now cracked and the dripper portion broke off years ago, but the clear, slightly sticky liquid itself is as pure today as it was on the day I carried it lovingly out of that spectacular Egyptian bazaar over 15 years ago.

The essence of the thing is exactly what that smart, sweet, toothless little magician of a salesman knew: the essence of a thing is the pure form of the thing. It is true and pure and lasts forever.

Heaven is full of exactly that: essence. Heaven is nothing BUT essences. And while I was in heaven, I, too, was the essence of myself. I was better, stronger, **more** than I had ever imagined myself to be. Everyone is.

All of "my particles" together with my consciousness were what I considered to be all of myself at that point. It was such that I felt and knew that all of these particles were, indeed, the essence of me and that my physical body had been a vessel to carry my essence while I had been on earth. I was essence energy and **entirely** complete with no body, and I felt I was in my true state in that place and form (or lack of form). I actually even somehow seemed more "me" there although there was less of me.

I felt more ME not because there was more of me. There wasn't. Rather, it was that what there *was* of me was somehow now in a higher/purer state of being. It was as if I had been distilled to only the purest and best parts of myself, and so I felt myself to be **more**. I was all that I had ever dreamed of being and then some!

So in the same way that the light felt to me that it was like light **plus**, I also felt like I was Leslie **plus**. Even though I was definitely minus a body, I was me **PLUS** while in heaven.

The feelings I experienced in heaven were also a *plus* version of feelings on earth. By that I mean that feelings were more intense there than any feelings I have known in this dimension.

In heaven, I experienced the essence of **all** the things I encountered. All things I encountered in heaven were in their/its highest/purest/truest form. Another way to say this would be that everything there is the best possible version of the thing. This very high state/frequency is the essence of what that thing truly IS. In heaven I experienced the essence of all that is.

Contrasted with the sheer intensity of everything in heaven, things on earth all seemed *diluted* when I first returned. I am much less aware of this now, but initially it felt to me almost like I was living in a watered-down version of reality here. I couldn't describe this odd sensation when I was first back in my body, and it frustrated me until I remembered Plato.

In a philosophy class I took at school, we had discussed the true nature of a thing, and I remembered that Plato had theorized that the ideal form or ultimate reality of a thing exists but that it does not exist in our daily lives.

The original form of the thing, in Plato's view, exists in some other (non-earth) realm. What we come into contact with in our lives on earth are merely illusions that are like replicas of the ideal and which have a limited life span. On the other hand, the essence or ideal of the thing is *eternal*. I remembered that when we had studied this in university, Plato's concepts had seemed to me unlikely at best.

After my near-death experience, I felt like Plato might have been closer to the truth than I'd given him credit for all those years ago. I continually felt like I was looking at faded versions or possibly "replicas" of pretty much everything that I encountered when I first got back to earth, and large parts of what Plato had theorized seemed to match with what I was now experiencing. Light, my own self, feelings: they all seemed somehow *less of all they could be* in the earth dimension than in heaven, and nothing on earth seemed to be in the highest/purest or "essence" form of the thing in the way it had been in heaven.

The aspect of this that was most striking to me was that I had never felt like things were replicas or diluted *before* my trip to heaven. But because in heaven I experienced everything at such a high vibration, the contrast between the two states was hard to miss upon returning.

Because we are in bodies here and require a lower frequency to hold the solid/liquid state, we are necessarily at a lower vibration on earth than in heaven, but we can all choose the highest possible vibration with each decision we make in this dimension and in this way we can choose to live at a very high frequency even while on earth. We are all MORE of all we can be when we are at a higher vibration. Life doesn't feel like it is "less than it could be" when we live in light and love on earth. We get closer to our essence by living this way.

Chapter 7

True Home

Heaven is like the Louvre for souls. It is filled with all sorts of masterpieces. Every piece there is the master, the original... the essence of the thing.

Because everything is the essence of the thing there, there is no possibility for anything to be less than all that it can be. Everything/everyone exists as the highest version of who they are in that place and so *everyone* is spectacular. Experiencing myself as the best version of myself felt amazing.

Additionally, every communication I was receiving was from the best and highest version of all of the other essences, and every act of communication felt clean, ultimately sincere and true. The communication felt sacred.

I both felt and also knew from the communications that this place was my true home. I knew it to be true that the Realm of Light is the eternal home and that the earth is only a temporary home.

The Realm of Light is not just true home for me, Leslie. It is True Home to all and for the essence of all. It is where *all* things already exist, the place from whence all earthly things originate, and the place where the essences "are".

The light communicated this information to me by flowing into and between and among and through every one of the particles of me while welcoming me home until I was humming with happiness and effervescing (imagine champagne bubbling!!) with joy.

I felt loved more than I had ever known was possible and the light kept telling me more and different exciting and wonderful things. My newfound knowledge/awareness together with all the magnificent feelings had me in a state something like an exuberant puppy who can't wait to experience whatever is next. I wanted to explore and play!!

While it may seem I have described a lot here, all of the things that had happened up to this point in the light seemed to me to happen in just a few moments.

Chapter 8

Exploring Heaven

And in the same way that it had (just moments earlier) seemed totally normal to find myself hovering up near the ceiling in an operating room, it now seemed completely normal that in the very instant I decided I wanted to explore and play, I began zipping around heaven.

Joy! Freedom! Yipppeeeeeeeeeeeeeeeeeee!!

Zooooom! Swish! Bo-innnnnnngggg!!

Imagine a spring bouncing all over the place. That was me. And the place I was bouncing all over?

Infinity!

I only needed to think of a place, and I was simply ....zoooooom!!!... IN that place. The experience was like a non-physical dessert of pure delight: perfect love infused with joy, frosted with the deliciousness of freedom.

Being able to think of any spot in that realm and then just kind of "pop" over there was exhilarating. One second you're here. Then the very next second... "POP", and now you're at the far reaches of the other side of beyond... simply because you thought it would be fun to explore this region --even though only a second ago you had been someplace *completely* different.

There was no need to use lots of time to move myself through space to get to another space. I had only to think of a location and then I would simply BE there--- *almost* instantly. I felt myself shooting to the new place. In fact, I felt kind of like a shooting star shooting off in one direction and then another. It was spectacular!

I was pure consciousness and my consciousness itself seemed to have the ability to be in one place or another. When I moved, it wasn't that I merely imagined going to a different place: I actually WENT there.

Initially, as I was doing this exploring, I maintained the configuration of the particles in loose cloud formation. The particles of Leslie all moved as a single entity.

Later I found another option. But that was later. Initially, the array of my particles didn't even really occur to me as something I could vary, so I just stayed in the form of a cloud because that was the configuration my particles had arrived in. It seemed to be something like my "default" mode.

After the welcome (...and possibly also at the same time as the welcome... Time is really different there...) Additional things were messaged to me and so my exploring phase included both travel and a form of education.

The information came in non-verbal/verbal/essence of meaning "packages", and with each new package of information I received, I felt and also intuitively understood/knew everything that was presented to me.

I grasped it all in all its full complexity down to the minutest detail. And this was done even more easily than we drink water when in human form. It seemed that I had access to all of the knowledge of heaven. I had only to think of a subject, and I knew of it completely and profoundly, yet simply and with no effort at all.

And so, I understood that this was my home and that this was heaven, and that the light all around me was made up of all that is and that I am also a part of all that is.

As before, I continued to feel that I was a part of heaven just as normally and naturally as any other part of heaven that was there. It seemed completely right and normal that this was what I was and what I was experiencing. None of it seemed the least bit shocking or in any way strange, and I had no thoughts whatsoever of earth or of my life there.

I knew I was Leslie, but I didn't think at this point about anything beyond me as the small cloud and being a part of the light. Leslie at the point only existed to me as that cloud of particles, and my only focus was zooming all over and learning everything about everything.

This exploration was completely joyful and perfect and normal, and I had never before felt so entirely in my element as I did then, yet there were no huge "AH-HA!!" moments. In a way, it was as if I was merely being reintroduced to things I already knew. It felt more like meeting back up with an old friend I hadn't seen in awhile than meeting a new friend.

It also felt to me it felt like this exploring was best thing I had ever done. EVER. I have no idea how long I spent 'bouncing' all over and checking out different things and having fun learning/remembering.

I was not exploring places on earth, by the way. I was checking out places in the Realm of Light (of which earth is not a part) and was learning how things in and out of the realm were all formed (they all came from the light) and what held it all together (love) and all about anything else that a soul might want to know.

Not only was I learning about everything. I was learning everything there is to know about everything....*all* about *all things* in greater detail than a person in a body could ever learn about even a single subject even if that person studied only one subject for an entire body-life on earth.

And all of this seemed, believe it or not, COMPLETELY normal --and none of the information felt wholly new or like I was learning it for the first time.

In a way, it was like I had just gotten home from a long trip and I was exploring my own house in the way I might if I had been gone from it for awhile and was now back and seeing things that I didn't remember when I was not at home… but now that I was back in the home certain things in it were special—even *dear* to me.

Have you ever done that? Been gone more than a few days and then came home and realized anew how much you love that little quirky thing (whatever it is) that you hadn't really even been conscious of before?

When that happens, we have an opportunity to see things that are not new in a kind of new way and enjoy all the things that make the house special. For example, maybe there is one handle on a door that wobbles just a little when you turn it and you only remember it when you touch that handle. But when you touch it, and that little wobble does its own unique little wobbly thing… you breathe a deep sigh and know you are really home.

Maybe you have been gone for a trip and get home and remember anew the way you fit so perfectly in that one special chair or the way your favorite crisp clean sheets smell and feel. Or maybe it's the way the water in your shower comes out of the shower head at that particular angle with that one little stream of water shooting off just a BIT too far to the left....but you had never been conscious of it until you were back home and back in the shower but then when you saw it you knew it had always been that way... but you just never remembered it before now.

Well... bouncing around and visiting the whole of the Realm of Light was kind of like that. It was as if I knew this entire place and all in it already but I didn't remember or appreciate that I knew it until I experienced it anew. Everything was spectacularly beautiful, and it was new to me in one way... but at the same time, none of it seemed really completely "new" to me and it was dear to me because it was part of me in some way.

And this just reinforced what I already knew: I was back in my true home.

Chapter 9

I Learn a New Trick

Now, as I said before, I had been in kind of a cloud formation (similar to a group of bees acting as a single entity when they form a cloud) while in the room above the table with the body in the earth dimension, and I generally maintained that same configuration of a cluster of particles while exploring.

I have no idea how long I spent exploring, but while I was not (and am not) clear about the length of time of this phase, I was very aware of my sense of self and the formation of my particles as I traveled in heaven.

It was as if I, Leslie, was also "we", the particles of Leslie, and it was this dual state We-Leslie who were/was doing the exploring. Each time I/we thought of a new place I wanted to go, I immediately zoomed there with all of my particles. There was an almost super-hero sensation of bolting off in the direction of my intended next stop and then ----vooooop!----- I'd be there almost immediately. Then, whenever I was ready for a new spot, I'd shoot off in a completely different direction to get to that next place.

It was exhilarating to feel my consciousness and my particles in one place and to then whisk away to another destination and in less than the time it would take to blink, be at that next position. During the time between being in Point A and arriving at Point B, it felt as if I was moving as light. I felt like 'me as particles' when I was more or less stationary, and then I felt like something akin to light when I was moving.

All of my 'me-ness' would stop immediately when we arrived at each new location within heaven, and in that instant of the stop, I felt like particles (rather than light) once again. While I was fully controlling *where* I was going, I did not seem to be controlling this particles-to-light-to-particles aspect of my experience. Instead, this just seemed to be happening: during that moment between locations I just *felt* myself existing as light (not particles), and then each time I stopped, I would suddenly notice myself existing as particles once again. However, no matter the form, I was always aware of myself as Leslie-consciousness, and I (Leslie) was completely free and able to travel anywhere within that realm just by intending to go there.

It is hard to know which pronouns to use as I describe all of this because while this was happening, I felt like I existed as both **we** (my particles) and as my individual self or **I** (my essence) at the exact same time. If I wanted to align the language here even more closely to my actual experience, I would consistently write **we/I** to describe myself when I was in heaven... but since that format clunks and bumps along awkwardly (at best!), I am instead switching between singular and plural pronouns from time to time in a way that is not commonplace. Interestingly, I suppose that in itself makes sense since nothing felt at all commonplace about heaven.

During this exploration segment of my time in heaven, it was clear to me that the intelligent light all around me was fully aware of all I was doing and it/they were completely fine with my explorations of what seemed to be a never-ending, light-filled expanse of unconditional love/light/intelligence.

Because I felt completely loved and free to do as I pleased, and because of the fun of it all, I moved all over heaven— like an exceptionally fast hummingbird covering huge expanses. Here, there, up, over, down, forward, back... now hovering again. I was exploring this and that and THAT and THIS --until somehow, I discovered a completely new and *different* thing that I could do.

I realized that here in the Realm of Light, in addition to the options of existing in a hovering formation as a cluster of particles or while moving as light—both of which involved keeping all aspects of myself more or less *together*-- there was another option: I could also send all of my particles out into separate *distant* positions. In other words, I could _disperse_ my individual particles! I was able to send each of the particles of myself to distinct places throughout the realm. I could disperse **throughout** heaven *and* maintain awareness of myself as ME.

I cannot overemphasize the amount of joy that accompanied this discovery.

My first thought: MORE FUN!!!!!!

And I immediately began to see how far I could go with this new trick.   There were seemingly no limits!

Where I had previously been sending all of the particles of myself --in a cluster-- to each new point of exploration and had been exploring spot after spot in that methodical way, I was now sending all of my particles outward in all directions so that they (and I!) could experience multiple *different* places ALL AT THE SAME TIME. This meant that I could be in many places simultaneously and also still be "me" as an individual consciousness. It was a spectacular discovery that allowed me to explore multiple points within heaven simultaneously.

When I dispersed in this way, I realized myself as more than merely the particles of Leslie/Leslie's essence. Certainly: I was still all of the particles of myself existing as Leslie (self), but because I was now also mingled in with all of the other particles of the WHOLE (all of heaven), I felt that I was at the exact same time also existing as *the whole*. In other words, I was **me** and I was also **me plus all the other particles** of heaven as well.

Say you drop a bit of green food coloring into a glass of water. Initially, the color will stay more or less together in a kind of clump of color. However, if you stir it, it will mix with the water until it is not possible to distinguish the green food coloring from the water. If you videotaped this and then played the video forward and backward, that is kind of like what I was doing.

I was mixing into heaven, but I could also --merely by desiring it to be so-- pull all of my particles back into a cluster of only me once again.

This allowed me to experience myself as me *and* as more than me. I maintained a complete sense of self. I had a complete blending with the whole as well.

Remember the commercial I described and they way all of the particles that came out of that single capsule spread out and floated in space? All of those floating particles in the commercial represent conscious particles and their consciousness constitutes my essence in heaven, but in heaven we also have all the particles from lots and lots of *other* capsules that are also all dispersed and intermingling, and all of these intermingled particles are filling all of the space in heaven.

As I looked at the other particles, even though I felt they represented individual essences, there was no visual representation of the individuals (as they had had when they existed in their individual capsules). This is precisely because in heaven all of the particles have come out from their capsules and are intermingled throughout the space of heaven. There is nothing remaining of any *physical* individuals... but the individual *consciousnesses* remain. Further, all of these particles are particles of light, so that if you look at this space from the outside, you don't even see any particles. All you see is light.

That describes very well where I was and what I was experiencing.

In the Realm of Light, specific particles are there that indeed were previously in different individual capsules (bodies). Even though these particles are now all intermingled, they *all* still maintain that individual sense of self (essence) which existed when they were each in separate bodies. They maintain awareness of themselves as that individual self which felt it was separate during the time in the capsule-- even while intermingled now in heaven. They each have a sense of individuality. Yet they also combine to form the whole.

They *are* the light in the Realm of Light...and I was a part of this as well!

These particles are particles that were in bodies that make up every imaginable bit of nature: rocks, trees, people, different animals, stars, you name it! And all of those things have different kinds of consciousnesses. Their "particles" are all merged in heaven and together they form the *all* in heaven. But they were also heaven *before* they ever went out from heaven into different physical forms.

I found myself now experiencing myself as a part of this larger **all** while still also being the aware of myself as the smaller **me**. It was indeed perfection. Unity. Freedom. Peace. Love.

Bliiiiiiiiiiiiiiiiiiiiiiiiiiiiiiiiiiiiiiiiiiiiiiiiiiiiiiiiiiiiiiiiiiiiiiiiiiiiiiiiiiiiiiiiiiiiiiiiiiii iiiiiiiiiiiiiiiiiiiiiiiiiiiiiiiiiiiiss.

It is really no great surprise that I thought this *dispersing my particles* ability which I had discovered was simply the coolest thing ever. With it, I could be me *and* be **all** at the same time. I could disperse my particles, or I could pull them all back to a single focused location. And I could switch between the two modes of my particles at will.

There was also the knowledge aspect of it! When I was in the expanded state of dispersed particles, I was still me, but I had access to **all** of the knowledge of all of the other particles that I was intermingled with. Ponder that for a moment.

Spectacular.

I gained the knowledge about everything that I was intermingled with each time I expanded out into the larger whole. Its knowledge became a part of my knowledge and understanding of *all that is.*

And in this way, I now understood more about the nature of the place I was in. I knew that all of the other particles in heaven were light particles of different individual essences— all intermingled, and that that is why at first they had felt like one thing existing as the light while I had also felt messages coming to me from individuals.

Now it was also evident to me that the light was not a solid blanket of light as it had first appeared...but rather the light of heaven itself was comprised of the particles of different essences, and because the essence of a thing is the highest and truest form of the thing, all of the light particles were all also love—because love is the highest and truest and purest aspect that exists. And so, the **all** of heaven (all that is) exists as light which is also particles of love and these particles that comprise heaven are the particles of the love of all. My particles were also love and also part of this **all**... AND I was still also Leslie-consciousness even when my particles were expanded and existing in this scattered-throughout-heaven state.

It was heavenly. ☺

This new "trick" allowed me to **fully** BE the ocean that I spoke of earlier while still also being Leslie. I was myself and was at the same time also fully integrated into the whole of the space that is the Realm of Light. I was not just IN heaven… I was also actually a PART of it. I could/would/did know all that the light knew. And I was still my own individual consciousness as well. I didn't blend in to the larger whole and lose my sense of self. Not at all. I blended, *and* I was still Leslie!

On top of that, the way my particles were pulling in together and then extending outward again and again had a kind of rhythm to it, so that it was almost as if I was breathing in when the particles contracted and then breathing out when the particles moved into the dispersed state.

This joyful, playful time of expanding and contracting my essence lasted for another length of unspecified time. It seemed to me that this went on for a fairly long period.

It was glorious, and I felt I could have gone on forever rhythmically "breathing" myself in and out while learning, reacquainting, exploring in this new way.

Chapter 10

I See Earth

But my playtime was interrupted when I looked down at one point and something caught my attention. It was just a speck – almost too small to notice—but for some reason I was curious about it.

The speck was definitely in a different realm, but it seemed "reachable" from where I was. As I looked at the speck, I felt a twinkling of recognition.

That speck is earth. Earth is where my body lived.

As I continued to look at the earth, I felt neutral about it in the way I had felt neutral about my body when I had seen it earlier. The earth appeared beautiful as I looked at it unemotionally. I had no memories of my time there at that point.

Since I have begun telling about my experience, people have asked me a lot about this part. They often ask if I tried to talk to any people on earth. I did not. However, some people from earth reached out to me and communicated with me.

62

The best way to describe this part of my experience is to go back to the idea of watching something on TV-- which I initially mentioned when describing myself as hovering over the table that my body was on during the operation.

When you are watching a TV program, it would never occur to you to try to have a conversation with the people on the TV. You can reach out and touch the TV if you choose, but the TV people are in a different dimension and you know this.

In a similar way, I could see earth, and it seemed "reachable" but it was evident that the earth was in a different dimension than I was. The beings on earth were in that same earth dimension.

I did not attempt to initiate communication with anyone on earth. The idea did not enter my thoughts. At that point, I didn't really have any concept of my life on earth. It only registered that my body had lived there.

As I initially looked down at earth, I contracted into my cloud-of-consciousness formation. As my consciousness remained focused on earth, I noticed myself "breathing" my particles in and out without consciously trying to do so. In this way, I experienced earth both from my contracted state and also from my expanded state.

There was a stark contrast between where I was in the light and the darkness surrounding the earth. The difference felt immense.

As I continued to focus on the earth, it "grew" before me from speck-sized to a small sphere that seemed to be about the size of a Christmas ornament. I then saw the whole planet as if it were an ornamental ball hanging on a huge Christmas tree that was from a huge forest--and the Realm of Light was that forest, and although the tree with its small ornament was no longer **in** the forest, I understood that the tree and the ornament were both *from* the forest.

I had a knowing through these symbols that the earth (ornament) and tree (darkness) were originally from the Realm of Light though not currently in the light... yet there was no actual tree or forest. These were just symbols that I saw and knew. In actuality, before me was only the earth, and it seemed to be hanging in darkness. All of that planet earth was inexplicably small compared to where I was.

Heaven seemed infinitely big compared to earth.

Even after the earth had zoomed up and was somewhat larger than the original speck I had noticed, it still felt far away from me because it was not in the dimension of light.

The planet was now before and below me. I saw/felt/knew that it was in a dimension where there was a lot of darkness and where things were in solid form. Where I was, nothing was solid in the sense that it is on earth, and there was also no darkness in the realm I was in. I was in a dimension of the most beautiful light and joy imaginable, so while earth looked lovely, I felt no pull toward it in any way whatsoever.

I felt the denseness of the earth contrasting with the lightness of where I was, and as I looked on noting the denseness of earth, all of a sudden there was a kind of burst of images that came up from the earth toward me. As this began, I contracted back to my cloud-of-particles formation, and I stayed in that configuration during this portion of my time in heaven.

Many, many different people in a wide array of emotional states and circumstances were flashing very, very quickly up to me, such that I found myself encountering what seemed to be thousands upon thousands of people in different situations and places on earth. I understood I was experiencing little snippets of these different people's lives in one possible version of the fairly near future.

All of this was "flashed" before me at such a fast speed that I had a hard time keeping up with it. I was certain at the time that I was I missing things because there was just SO much being shown to me, but I felt the emotions of the people very deeply and I understood that I was being shown people currently or soon to be on earth. Some of them I recognized. Most of them I didn't feel I knew, but I understood that Leslie on earth had either *had* or *would have* some connection with them all at some point if this possible future came to pass. I was shown what each person was doing and what each of them was feeling during the little blip I got of each person.

This was not a peaceful experience. The way the images and emotions were kind of spurting up at me seemed far too fast and direct. There were emotions of extreme joy but also of boredom and failure, sadness, darkness, and even despair. Everything was supercharged emotionally, and each different person's segment flew up to me from the earth separately. They flew up from all around the globe.

Visually, it was somewhat like when I had first tried to shuffle a deck of cards by splitting the deck into two halves and then bending the cards to make a bridge, but I messed up and all of the cards went flying everywhere. Here though, instead of cards flying all out of control, there were these little flying videoettes spewing emotions. And they were all zooming up from earth. Toward me.

While I felt the individual segments pelting into me almost like a hard rain, because of the raw nature of the undiluted feelings and because of the way the images and emotions came at me, it was actually even more powerful than the feeling of rain hitting my consciousness. I felt like I was being hit with water from a fire hose. Because the majority of the emotions were so intense and at such a different vibration than I was, they actually *hurt* as they collided with my consciousness.

After some time, it began to slow down-- much the way the water from a hose slows but continues to come out for a bit after the water itself is turned off. The stream gradually tapered until no more image/emotion pieces were flying up at me.

Although the show was over, I was transfixed. Exhausted. Pondering it all.

It felt as if, through these pictorial/emotional bursts in which I had been shown a segment of each of these people's lives and emotions, I was somehow now bonded to all of these people in a new way. I felt I was missing a lot of information though, and I couldn't name the actual nature of the bond. It was all very confusing and overwhelming.

Even so, I understood the overarching message which was that these were situations and things that would likely play out if I went back to earth... That I could help with some of the sadness I was seeing and also be the bringer of some of the joy I was witnessing—for these thousands of people.

I had formerly had no idea that my life on earth had touched or would or ever *could* touch so many. In this moment, it was made known to me that it is by no means necessary for an individual to touch another life intentionally or directly in order to make a huge difference in that life-- and that this is a truth for all of us. Everything we do, everything we feel, and everything we think has a far greater impact than most on earth know.

It seemed that I could make a net positive impact if I returned to earth.

And I was then made aware that I was being given a choice.

I could go back to earth, or I could stay in the light.

As I looked on and contemplated this, I saw the earth go back to the size of a speck. Then, before me a figure zoomed up from earth. This person was someone I knew, and he didn't slam into me as the others had. It was an old and dear earth friend, and he stopped in the dark space without coming all the way to me in the light.

Although I was still in the realm of light and he was not in the dimension of light, he was very near the light and he was close

68

enough that I could see him clearly. He looked exactly as I knew him to look on earth except that he was hovering in space now. I knew him and felt my love for him as a friend although I still didn't remember my life on earth. I heard him easily as he began to speak.

He called out to me by name and then pleaded with me to come back to earth. His message was very short but heartfelt. The impact on me was powerful.

Immediately after that, the man I was dating at the time was suddenly floating in the space above earth, too. He was suspended next to my dear friend in the darkness.

He and I had not been dating more than a few weeks, and I somehow knew that as soon as I saw him-- although I still knew essentially nothing about my life back on earth. I remember initially being quite surprised that he chose to communicate with me because I felt like we barely knew each other. Upon having that thought, I was "told" and I could "see" we had a soul connection and this was a soul issue which had no relationship to the length of time we had known each other on earth.

My then-boyfriend took his cowboy hat off and waved it back and forth as if trying to get my attention. He pleaded for me to come back to earth, and then my friend joined back in so that the two of them were briefly hovering next to each other (but in their own separate little bubbles of that dimension of darkness) before me. Both were both begging me to come back to earth. I did not get the impression that either knew the other was there.

I still couldn't fully comprehend exactly what they meant by "come back" to earth. But I knew they wanted me to go to the realm they were in.

I watched all of this, but while I felt the emotions intensely, I was at the same time also somehow unattached to it all. It seemed to me that the realm of light was where I was supposed to be. I had no desire to "go back" to my body on earth—whatever that actually entailed. It wasn't that I was denouncing earth. I was just certain that I wanted to stay in the light and since earth was not in the dimension of light, I did not want to go there.

I started in heaven/home with no body. I went to earth and lived in a body. The body died. I continued to live with no body. I came back to heaven/true home.

It seemed simple enough to me. I was back in my true home now. Why would I ever want to leave? No one was going to convince me to leave this place...

Or were they?

Chapter 11

All That Is Isn't **ALL THAT IS**

In order to explain how this next part happened, it is first necessary to give a fuller description of where I was in relationship to other things at this point because this next part was the most moving part of my entire experience in that dimension, and to grasp it fully the visuals need to be clear.

I have already said that I was in what felt like an expanse that was as big as all of *all that exists*. The expanse was heaven which I experienced as the realm of the most radiant and loving light I had ever known. The light was made up of intelligent love which was the essence of everything and all things, and this love was visible as the whitest of any light I had ever seen. It was sometimes particles of information and was also sometimes flowing and moving, and it was always somehow both. If I tried to draw a picture of the dimension I was in, it would be infinitely huge and it would look like there was really nothing to see in heaven except that soft, beautiful, all-loving light.

I had never imagined anything so amazing could exist... and that is exactly why what happened next was so astonishing.

As all of my particles were still focused in the direction of earth, the conscious light that I was hovering within was continuing to send non-stop flows of love to me. I noted again that the earth looked very, very, very small compared to where I was. It was like the tiniest imaginable blip in a huge expanse of darkness. In contrast, as I breathed myself out again into my state of expanded particles, I knew that I was as infinite as all of heaven. There was no sense of grandeur or ego in this feeling. It was merely an observation of fact. And as I looked down and saw earth below me, smaller than small, I was emotionally neutral and simply observing the fact that heaven felt infinite and the earth felt inexplicably tiny.

And then, everything changed.

A light appeared from behind me that was so large that (even in my expanded state of being as big of all of heaven!!) I now I felt myself and all of heaven to be extremely small.

Not only was this approaching light infinitely larger than all of heaven. The *quality* of this light was also different than the light that I was now a part of. The love and beauty of this newly arrived light coming from behind me far surpassed the love of the light that I was a part of.

Additionally, the light I had been in while in heaven up to this point had come to feel to me as many essences "mingled" together and being expressed as one, and I was a part of this one. But this new and approaching light was also a completely different kind of light in that it felt to me like ONE essence instead of being made up of huge quantities of different essences all intermingled.

I slowly turned my consciousness away from the earth and toward this breathtaking light. And while I almost could not believe it was possible, the approaching light was not only infinitely larger than all of the Realm of Light, it also felt like **ALL** rather than *all*. Heaven had felt like all. This felt like MUCH more than all. This felt like it was the ***ALL*** that *everything else* comes from.

The light now approaching me also felt even more love-filled and sacred, and was simply more spectacular in every imaginable way than the light I was already in. This light was somehow even more grand than heaven itself.

As I turned and looked at this still-approaching light, I knew immediately: this is GOD. This most loving of all possible lights was GOD himself expressing himself to me AS LIGHT.

GODLIGHT is too spectacular for me to ever hope to adequately describe. I *can* say this about my first moment in that light, however. All of the Realm of Light that I had previously thought to be ALL OF HEAVEN and ALL THAT IS, was now dwarfed by this now-approaching light which was somehow even more light-filled than the already indescribably spectacular (which I had previously thought to be the most beautiful ever) light which I was in myself. Heaven (where I was) in comparison to GODLIGHT, now seemed as small as the earthspeck had previously seemed in comparison to heaven.

My first reaction was to bow every one of my particles in utter reverence.

Chapter 12

GODLIGHT

The size, glory, radiance and indescribable holiness that was this light which now came toward me filled me with complete AWE.

The peace, joy, truth, sacredness, and unconditional love of this divine light shone on me so that I was like a flower in the sun. Dancing with happiness. Every last one of my particles swirling with bliss. *Completely* in awe.

Just as I knew immediately that this was the essence of what I had always called GOD, I also understood that no name in an earthly language can ever fully capture this essence.... This was all of all that is love. This was ALL of all in the Realm of Light. This was and is and always will be ALL of ALL.

And here I was in the presence of this light. And its attention was focused on me.

ME!!! Before GOD in the form of LIGHT.

During my explorations earlier here in the realm of light, I had been told/shown and had learned that light is love and love is all. It therefore seemed fitting and perfect for GOD to be expressing himself in the form of light/love. I instantly thought of him as GODLIGHT.

I use different names to refer to this light/him/her/ALL/God/GOD/the fount from which all things come. Any name in earthly language will limit this unlimited essence and it is likewise not possible to adequately describe the abundance of love and peace that flow outward from this source, this fount from which all flows. The main reason I so often use the term "GODLIGHT" when describing that which is often called GOD is simply because that is how he/she/ALL/Fount felt to me: God in the form of light. The name is not important. Whatever name we give it/her/him/them/all…. This essence remains ALL and LOVE is the essence of ALL.

GODLIGHT continued to approach slowly- giving me time to prepare myself for this experience, I imagined- until he reached me, all the while shining love down onto little me. When he was before me, as he shone upon me, he put what seemed like gigantic light-arms with "sleeves" like sheets of light around me so that it was almost as if I was being swaddled in his LIGHT/LOVE.

I was a tiny speck now in these magnificent "arms" of most-sacred light. The light wrapped around me, but it also emanated out from GODLIGHT in all directions infinitely. The arms were not anything like physical arms, but I use this term because although we were both in bodiless states, I felt I was being held. The purity, compassion, respect, peace, joy, and infinite *depth* of the love in which I was being held cannot be overemphasized. I was enveloped in GODLIGHT's strong, all-encompassing love and I blissfully basked in the glorious feeling!!

The effect was like a huge womb made of the lightest of light-filled loves imaginable. And while this was all *around* me -at the same time- it was as if light was being breathed into me gently but in massively huge quantities. I was also being bathed in and absorbing the unconditionally perfect love of GODLIGHT himself.

This flowing of the love to me... in such massive quantities... in combination with the feeling of being held this way was spectacular! I was in GODLIGHT's embrace. As a child is held by its parent, I was being held by GODLIGHT and nothing else mattered. I was complete in every way.

Each time I think of it now, I overflow anew with joy. This was the most wonderful moment of my time in heaven up to that point.

But then it got EVEN BETTER!!!

After some time of holding me, GODLIGHT spoke.

He said only one word.

He said

..... my name.

Gulp.

GODLIGHT knows my name. GOD KNOWS MY NAME!!!!!!!

As quickly as this thought began resonating through me, immediately an answer resonated back with strength and such a quantity of unconditional love that I was beyond a state of bliss. The answer was more beautiful than the most beautiful sunset ever seen. The answer that came back was simple and true:

I KNOW THE NAMES OF ALL. YOU ARE PART OF THE ALL. EACH PART OF THE ALL HAS UNTOLD VALUE AND I KNOW EACH PART OF EACH PART.

Below is what was happening at the forefront of my consciousness while that was spoken:

Have you ever stood in a mountain stream in the springtime? It is spectacular, is it not?

The water is freezing cold and it makes you feel really alive! It is clear and seems *somehow* completely different from water anywhere else. All you have to do is compare that from-the-mountain-spring water with bottled water, and you will feel the difference instantly.

Both are water, certainly. Yet the mountain-stream water (especially from *very* high up in the mountain) somehow feels MORE fresh than bottled water does. Plus, that water just sitting in a bottle is not flowing. Streams flow, and the flowing makes a difference in how we experience the water. Though both are water, they are quite different. A part of that difference is in whether the water has been flowing or not flowing. Hmmmmmmmmmmmm.

GODLIGHT held me and flowed love to me.

I felt GODLIGHT was transferring thoughts to me through the light. These thoughts then immediately became the things I was thinking about:

This flowing aspect is very important. But it is not the flowing of water that we are concerned with here. It is the flowing of love. Yes. And this IS the source on the mountaintop from whence all flows outward. The thing that is flowing outward here is love. And love transitions into all things of the universe. GOD is love flowing-- and GOD is also the fount from which LOVE flows! This is where LOVE originates. This is the source of all that is, and all that is IS MADE OF LOVE. Yes...I understand now. Everything – not just in heaven but everything everywhere is made of love. And this is the source of that love. This is the source of all. This is ALL. LOVE is all. Love flows out from this source. There is a never-ending supply of love here. There is always more love. This flowing love is life. Life is flowing love. Flowing love is living!

And with that I began flowing love consciously back to GODLIGHT. And he was pleased that I had learned another trick.

The light was a medium for communication as well as being light and love.

I was thinking many different things at the time I was being held by GOLDIGHT because I was getting lots and lots of different messages from his/her/its light all at once. The above is *one* stream of thought I was having while I was being held before the "official discussion" began.

During this period of being held, at times I wasn't sure if the thoughts I was thinking were my own thoughts or if they were the thoughts of GODLIGHT that I was receiving. This oddity from an earthly perspective was perfectly normal in that place and time. And it was possible because upon getting any message from GODLIGHT during this part of the being-held phase, I immediately knew the message to be true and it became a part of me, and the time between GODLIGHT sending a message and me getting it and processing it was so small that it felt it did not exist at all-- and that is how I was and am not not sure which thoughts I thought after I got a message from GODLIGHT and which thoughts were thoughts that GODLIGHT told me and then I adopted them as truths.

My thoughts were fast-- yet somehow also almost happening in slow motion at the same time. Everything was really clear to me as well, and each new thought felt like its own little epiphany and this one little pathway of my thinking continued on something like this:

This love is like that water --fresh and clear-- from the top of the mountain. **(AHHH-HAAAAA!)** It is pure and fresh and flowing joyfully. ALL LOVE STARTS HERE. Just as water in a mountain stream and bottled water are both water, love is love... but this love is purer because it is directly from the fountainhead and also because it is flowing forth freely and not being held in a container...

And it is being flowed to me (me!!!!!) in massively huge quantities! **(BASKING!!!!)** This love flowing to me is coming directly from the fount where love originates...GODLIGHT is the ORIGIN of LOVE. **(I KNEW THIS STUFF BEFORE!!!)** The flowing gives it life, is life, life is love flowing. **(YES!! YES!! YES!!!!)**

And this clear, fresh, mountain spring love in the form of light rushed into me swiftly. Flowing to me joyfully, it came to me carrying messages, and the clarity and truth of the messages were warm and perfect.

This went on for an unspecified period of time. It seemed to last a long time but not nearly as long as I would have chosen for it to last. (I wanted it to last forever.)

Eventually, I sensed a slowing in the messages although the love continued to flow. My own thoughts slowed as the messages slowed, until I felt and thought only this:

LOOOOOOOOOOOOOOOOOOOOOOOOOOOOOOOOOOOOOOOOO OOOOOOOOOOOOOOOOOOOOOOOOOOOOOOOOOOOOOOOOO OOOOOOOOOOOOOOOOOOOOOOOOOOOOOOOOOOOOOOOOO OOOOOOOOOOOOOOOOOOOOOOOOOOOOOOOOOOOOOOOOO OOOOOOOOOOOOOOOOOOOOOOOOOOOOOOOOOOOOOOOOO OOOOOOOOVE.

LOOOOOOOOOOOOOOOOOOOOOOOOOOOOOOOOOOOOOO
OOOOOVE.

Ahhhhhhhhh! Love!

My heart was full and at peace.

Then, for just a moment, like when you are swinging high on a swing and it reaches the highest point and then stops there at the apex for just a *split* second- suspended in perfection- before it starts to fall back toward earth again... for the very briefest of moments, I felt everything stop.

There was complete stillness in my heart. Everything was perfect.

PERFECTION.

But only for an instant.

Because in next moment, it was as if that swing moved again. And with that movement, I remembered everything about my life on earth.

Chapter 13

The Abyss

My parents had wanted a large family, but after my older sister had been born, my mom had had several miscarriages and the doctor/s told her she would likely not have any other children. When I was born, my parents were elated. My mom often told me this story and she ended the story by telling me that my being born was a miracle for her and my dad. There is a family photo that someone snapped at the exact moment my dad told my older sister (who was then six years old) that I had been born. The joy on both of their faces says everything about how much I was loved.

Yet I could not, for some reason, accept this love.

My parents had two additional children (my brother and younger sister) after I was born, and my mom and dad loved us and gave their hearts and souls to us. I had had a beautiful childhood in terms of what was going on in the environment around and outside of me. The problem I had been dealing with was something that was entirely INSIDE of me. And it felt to me as if it had been with me since birth.

I had, from as early as I could remember, always felt there was something seriously wrong with me at the core. In fact, I was positive that I was innately defective at the level of my soul. The way I saw it was that on the outside, I seemed normal. I could pass as normal. But on the inside, I knew I was broken —and had been from day one. I had come off the assembly line with a serious imperfection.

This serious imperfection manifested in what I later came to call "the abyss", although for many years I had no name for it. Though it was unnamed, this thing-- and the fear of this thing-- impacted every thought that led to every action in my life.

The abyss was a horrible, black void of nothingness that seemed to simply sneak into me from out of nowhere and then open up inside of me. Each time it came, I fell away from myself. It was like a sinkhole within me that robbed me of my heart. I felt my soul was broken when this happened. How else could it fall out of me?

The void didn't only take my heart. It took everything that was in my chest cavity so that all that remained was the lack. Each time it returned, I felt my insides suddenly disappear into a bottomless chasm of *nothing* leaving only the huge void within me. My brain remained in my body and simply observed the stillness and emptiness of my body sans soul.

The abyss feeling could hit me at any moment, and this *IT-can-happen-anytime- and-anywhere* aspect of it all left me feeling extremely vulnerable because I never knew when *it* would appear. Incidentally, this is clearly the same feeling of powerlessness that terrorists have chosen to use to create a sense of fear in the masses. It is extremely effective at creating fear because if you never know when something horrible might happen, you can never *really* feel safe. This means you can never let your guard down.

Living that way was an exhausting way to live. If you live like this, you are **always** afraid because the next moment or the next or possibly the *next* or the moment *after* the next or maybe even possibly the moment *following* the moment of that next moment or really at **any** moment (you can see how the mind gets obsessed with this!!) at any time of the day or night *it* could suddenly strike. And--- *Zuuuuuuuuuuuup!* Just like that, your heart is in the abyss and you are cold on the inside where your *you-ness* used to be.

The empty feeling of the abyss, the feeling that I was defective because of it, and that feeling that since I never knew when it would come, I was never safe were all compounded by the fact that I was certain no one else had an abyss, and so I felt very alone and I knew I could tell no one since I was the only one that had this horrible defect and if

86

anyone found out how messed up I truly was deep down on the inside, they would stop loving me and abandon me.

Of course, now I know I am not defective at all—no one is. I am not worse than anyone else. I am not better than anyone else. I have value simply by virtue of the fact that I exist. We all do! But back then... Back then, I had a very different perspective on life. I felt I was worthless because I believed I had a soul defect, and the fear that I was going to be "found out" to be the worthless person I believed myself to be was with me at all times.

Whenever people said something like *it's what's on the inside that counts*, my stomach would start to get all bound up. I knew that was probably true and it only confirmed what I already knew: I was worthless.

Sometimes I wondered where the abyss went was it wasn't in me. I thought maybe it kind of traveled around and was opening up in other people when it wasn't in me. But then I decided that if that was the case, other people would surely be talking about it... right?

But no one ever mentioned anything about anything even *remotely* like an abyss, so I knew I was the only one that had this defect. When it happened, I was reminded that I was not like other people. Other people were normal on the inside.

Not me. I was normal on the outside, but I was defective at the core.

One of the reasons I have decided to share my experience is because I now realize there may well be people out there right now who feel they are in some way or another defective and who may be living in fear as I was. My gut tells me that some of the people whose emotions were spurting up at me from earth might be people that fall into this category, and I want everyone to know that heaven's perspective allows us to see that no one is defective and that there is no need to feel unworthy—not ever.

But back then, I didn't know that.

From my earliest memories, I recall fearing that if others found out I was defective, they would no longer love me and they would abandon me-- and I would be left completely alone. At a very young age, I made a decision to not let anyone know about my secret, my defect.

Much of my personality was molded by the abyss and my fears. Because I was always secretly afraid of being abandoned by the people I loved most (if they ever found out the truth about me), I went out of my way to be extra good in every way I knew so that no one would ever be able to guess how messed up I was on the inside. People have since told me they thought I was sweet, but I thought I was a fraud.

My relationships with others were generally not very deep or healthy. How could they be? I didn't feel I deserved anyone's love. On top of that, no matter what others said or did, I knew there was always going to be a barrier between me and them because I would never tell my secret. I wanted to tell someone... but I was too afraid.

My mom used to lead us in prayers at bedtime. My younger brother and I shared a room for a few years (I think up until around the time I went to kindergarten) so we said our bedtime prayers together at that point. After we said our prayers out loud, I always added in lots of extra prayers quietly in my heart trying to name every single person that I knew and even adding in groups of people I hadn't met. I had heard about a big place called China. Since it was big, I thought maybe they had a lot of people, so I always included "and all the Chinese" in my prayers. When I prayed silently in those moments, what I asked was for God to bless all of the people I loved and all of the people I didn't know—basically all the people on earth-- so that they wouldn't ever be broken like I was and so the abyss would never enter any of them.

There were lots of times, before I fell asleep at night, when I wondered if my little brother also had the abyss. I came so close to asking him many, many times... but I never did. He didn't seem defective at all. He was so wonderful and loving. He was such a great brother and person. But maybe he was just pretending to be normal (like I was) and maybe he really had the abyss, too? But then again, maybe not... and if I let him know I was broken, he might not love me anymore. I would fall asleep wishing I could tell him.

In the beginning, if the abyss ever arrived during the day, it would stay with me all day. When I fell asleep it would always disappear.

There was a dream I used to have a lot as a child. In this dream, I was flying. When I flew, I knew that I was amazing and powerful-- and not defective. I used to wake up in the mornings after the flying dream and wish it was the reality.

My mom is Italian American and I was raised Catholic. One Sunday, we went to church after the void had already opened up inside of me. As I sat in church that day, I could not focus on the mass because of the void. Instead, I prayed for God to bring back my heart and to close the void. (I think I must have been about six at the time.) I felt God come into my heart in that moment. It was as if God had brought my heart back to me... and the void closed.

But it only closed temporarily. The abyss still returned often. The good thing was that I now knew that if I prayed with everything I had, the abyss would always close.

All of this led me to have lots of questions about God because I knew from my personal experience that God answered prayers-- but my experience with God closing my void seemed very, very different from what people were doing and talking about at church.

While I believed in God, I prayed to God mainly just in two ways: 1) asking that he would keep the void away from everyone else and bless everyone I loved and everyone on earth, and 2) asking him to take a moment when he had a free second to pretty please close my abyss -yet again. I would always tell him I was sorry for the inconvenience of asking him for his help with this second part.

As I got older, I explored many different religious views. Although I loved GOD with all my heart, I never really felt any singular religion was the right fit for me. I felt my defect made me unworthy of God's love.

By the time I became an adult, the abyss itself only came a few times a year. I had found that if I kept my mind busy, it did not enter me. For that reason, I did everything possible to keep my mind occupied.

My parents are both avid readers and our home was filled with books, so reading was a natural hobby for me to pick up —and it just happened to keep the abyss away as well. Any moment when I might otherwise have been alone with myself, I would get my mind busy and read. I myself became an avid reader at a very young age partly because of this.

I had other interests, too. I had a passion for language in general as well as for anything "international". I quickly learned that books took me to faraway places and gave me the new perspectives I yearned for. I loved maps (especially old ones) and collected foreign coins, and when I was in first and second grade, I dreamed of being an explorer/cartographer who sailed around the world on my sailboat mapping out new places and writing about my discoveries during the day and then reading books all night long. I saw all the blue on the globe and imagined there must have been lots of undiscovered land still out there in what people just mistakenly thought was open ocean. I was more than a bit bummed when I learned that all the continents had already been discovered.

I devoured everything that had print on it or in it. And always, deep in my heart, I held the hope that I might someday find someone, somewhere through *something* I read, who had dealt with the same kind of defective soul issue that I had.

I also loved to write. And while I had no confidence in myself about writing (or anything else for that matter) I simply loved playing with words the way writing allowed me to do. If I couldn't be a cartographer, I'd be a writer. When I wrote, I felt whole. There was no hole.

Have you ever thought about what you'd do if you got three wishes? I've always thought that if we could see what a person would wish for, we'd know a lot about that person. Anyway, if I had been handed a "one wish for free" ticket as a child, I would have had an inner battle between wishing to not have the abyss or wishing for world peace. They seemed equally important to me. In fact, I wished for one of those two things every year when I blew out my birthday candles. I had also decided that if I ever won the "wishes-granted lottery", after the void was banned and world peace was established, I would wish to be a writer. That's how much I loved writing.

So, for one of my general education classes during my first year at university, I decided to take a semester of writing. To say the least, I was thrilled about being in my first-ever official writing class.

My professor for that class, Dr. Laura Weaver, was (and is!) wonderful. Of course, I was completely nervous around her because I felt I wasn't good enough to deserve her time and help. But I will forever be thankful to her for her persistence in making sure I knew that she saw a spark of something special in my writing. In fact, before we were barely into the semester, she sat me down and told me that she thought I should consider becoming a writer. A bubble of happiness grew in my heart as she talked with me about my strengths.

I was ecstatic. It was my grandest dream to be a writer, and I was thrilled that she thought I had the talent to be one. A bubble of happiness was burgeoning within me.

But then reality hit me: I was too afraid to actually go for my dream.

And with that realization, I watched my dream deflate. The joy from inside the happiness bubble leaked out into and was lost within the fear surrounding it, until my happiness bubble was completely gone, and the abyss was back.

From that point forward, I then also hated myself for being a coward. I think it was around this time that I decided that while I loved children, I would not have any children because I felt it would be better for a child to remain unborn than to have me as a mother.

I ended up majoring in English Literature. It seemed a comfortable fit for a woman who read continually, and I felt much more at ease reading great authors than creating something of my own that could (and surely would) be rejected.

By the time I was in my thirties, I had pretty much *consciously* forgotten about the actual abyss. I had found tactics to keep it away, but underneath I was still certain I was defective. And since I could never find the confidence to share with anyone about my "soul defect" I could never really be close to anyone.

I had gotten married at 26. We had a beautiful wedding ceremony --during which I cried non-stop with the fear that that this man I wanted to share everything with would one day discover I was defective and hiding it from him and then leave me.

After we were married, I went into a deep depression because I wanted to tell him the truth about myself but was too much of a coward to tell even my own husband about my defect. My hate for myself grew. I felt unworthy of being married to a good man.

Not surprisingly, I was divorced by the age of 29. I wanted to be married, but I didn't even know how to have a loving relationship with myself. I tried dating after my divorce, but that was equally painful. And while I felt my family's love and also had friends who I knew loved me, I didn't feel worthy of any of them.

It wasn't only people I felt unworthy of. I also felt I was unworthy of anything that I deemed even remotely good. As an example of this, eating was a huge problem for me. Much of the time I would gag while trying to eat -- because I did not even feel worthy of *food*.

There *was* one part of my life I felt great about. That was my work life. After graduation, I had taken my first job working overseas teaching English as a Second language in Japan, and I had been working with adult students of English from around the world ever since. When I was teaching language to my international students, I forgot about being unworthy and lived joyfully. I loved my work.

But outside of anything related to my work, I was pretty much convinced that everyone and every *thing* was more valuable than I was, and there were times when I felt I could not go on. Often, especially at these times, when things got so horrible that I felt I could not stand it anymore, there was an amazing light that would come to me out of nowhere and shine its love on me.

That light felt like unconditional love holding me, and it made me feel better whenever it came. I never understood where that light was coming come from. But now I had a feeling I was about to find out.

96

Because … now???!

NOW? Where am I now? Oh, yes.

I am in heaven!!

For a second I almost forgot where I was because I received all of this data about myself in such a way that I somehow "re-experienced" it happening to me. This all happened very, very fast so that in no time at all I had both relived and also seen my life on earth. During this playback, I had been held by GODLIGHT and had been looking at earth the same time.

My choices in my life on earth life had been dominated by feelings of unworthiness and fear of abandonment that stemmed from the fear of my defect being discovered.

Yet while in heaven…

….in heaven… I knew I had no defect!

This changed EVERYTHING!!!

I rang like a bell with happiness because I knew the truth of heaven was the reality. Somehow it had seemed like I had had a defect on earth… but from heaven I could see that had just been an illusion. It was clear from where I was in heaven looking down to earth and seeing my earth life that I actually had no defect whatsoever.

From GODLIGHT's perspective, I am perfect and so is everyone and everything. From heaven I can see that I am good. I am love. We are all good. We are all love.

And GODLIGHT loves me. HE LOVES ME! He loves **all** of me! I am worthy of God's love!

GODLIGHT loves me through and through and through and through and through for all eternity.

I was being hugged and loved by Godlight and for the first time I also loved myself. I hugged my non-physical self. Then I beamed love/light back to Leslie in all of those difficult moments on earth, too.

When I sent love back to myself in earlier difficult situations on earth, I seemed to have reached a level of understanding that Godlight was pleased with. I felt his joy for me and for what I had now understood.

What I had grasped was not only that we are all perfect and we are all love but also that love is light AND love is not bound by time as we tend to think of time on earth. In fact, time is not at all what most people on earth think it is. This means that love in the form of light can be sent to the "past" or the "future" version of ourselves or another. This is possible if we understand this and choose this.

GODLIGHT then explained more to me in fuller detail about the light that I had received on earth all of those times when I felt I could not go on another moment. In those moments, when that heavenly light appeared, that light was none other than the light from ME, Leslie!! That love-filled, beautiful light that had arrived out of nowhere and had so often closed the void/carried me through my most difficult times... *that* magnificent light had been sent from Leslie (post heaven visit) to Young Leslie—the struggling pre-heaven-visit Leslie of the past.

To put it more precisely, I had actually sent Godlight's love- which had been given to me- outward from me in the form of light back through time to earlier versions of myself.

With this knowledge- that I have no defect and that I, in fact, had been the one sending myself light all along, I decided I had a whole lot more to learn.

I sent a love-filled message of light to GODLIGHT: Please teach me more!!

And from there began the discussion between

GODLIGHT and a beaming little me.

Chapter 14

Why Souls Choose Challenges

Our discussion began with a continuation of the topic that had dominated my life on earth until that point. I understood that GODLIGHT began with this topic since it was the most active question/issue within me at that moment.

ALL that exists has/have value. There is no separate one. Each is part of the WE. All are a part of ALL. WE are ALL ONE.

ALLONE IS/HAS VALUE just by means of its/our/your existence.

I never felt valuable before. What a remarkable way to look at things.

... But I am still not clear about why I was born with a defect.

THERE ARE NO BIRTH DEFECTS FROM MY PERSPECTIVE, and I can see all. You are perfect. Everyone is perfect if we look from the perspective of heaven.

Wow. I love this way of seeing things.

You are whole and complete and perfect unto yourself. You are also a perfect part of the larger whole as well. This is true for each being on earth.

If you do not see yourself as complete and perfect and also see that the entire whole (all that exists) is also complete and perfect, it is only that your perspective is not allowing you to see the larger truth.

From heaven's vantage point, it is easy to see that each of you is a part of the divine whole as well as being complete unto yourself. This is true for all.

Yes. I see that-- and know that to be true.

You existed, as you exist now, before you went to earth. You knew these larger truths that can be seen from this vantage point at that time. And from this place, you made a choice to go to earth with what you have been calling "a defect".

I understand that it felt to you like you were not perfect on earth, but this is only because you <u>chose</u> for it to feel this way before you went to earth.

You/all (all souls) want to intentionally create scenarios that will allow you to have certain specific types of experiences while on earth.

These experiences are things that your soul wants to have because they are related to the things that your soul is interested in, and so your essence (you) desired to create aspects of your earth life that would bring about certain types of experiences.

As a catalyst for these experiences, you each pick specific parameters for your life on earth: your family, your environment, your physical attributes, and any changes to what are by most on earth considered the "normal" physical, mental, or emotional construction/balance of beings while on earth.

You choose these things intentionally BEFORE you go to earth.

There are no mistakes: you chose your "abyss" for a specific reason.

There are no mistakes: you each choose your earth family and they choose you.

Each of you feels a love and desire to explore certain things on earth because these are things your soul is interested in.

In fact, that thing that you considered a defect while on earth was actually chosen very carefully for you by you yourself after consultation with your 'heaven team' because you all agreed it would be a wonderful tool to have on earth to help you move toward your soul's interest.

It was the opposite of a defect. It was planned in advance.

Your soul's interest is one of the reasons you wanted to leave heaven and go to earth in the first place, and this thing you have called a defect was actually something chosen for you and *by* you to help you with your soul's interest. You knew (before going down to earth while still in heaven) that it would be a great challenge to have the abyss, and you were excited about it the way explorers are excited about exploring uncharted regions or in the way that some people are fascinated with climbing mountains.

You chose to have the abyss come to you so that you could experience a very different and special way of BEing in the earth dimension. Others choose other things. You each choose the kinds of things you choose in order to have a specific kind of challenge. From the perspective of heaven, this is an adventure and you know it will be challenging but will also be fun in the way that climbing a mountain is challenging and fun for a mountain climber.

Each person's particular challenge is also a part of that essence's soul interests on earth and beyond earth. Some choose to be blind or to be born to a difficult family situation... there is an endless list of the challenges and combinations of challenges that a soul can choose to have in an earth life. These challenges are often things that you are born with or that appear fairly early in life and are with you in the formative years on earth. These are not mistakes although from the perspective of the earth dimension you may believe otherwise.

Every soul desires the feeling of grappling with something—and then overcoming that thing (whatever that thing is). Continuing to choose love no matter what circumstance/s your challenge has given you leads to overcoming the challenge.

Taking on such challenges gives you the opportunity to experience things from a different perspective than you would have without the challenge. This is great fun for your soul—even though it may not feel like fun for you in your earth life if you do not understand that you (and your family) chose this situation intentionally.

If you move through this challenge while continually flowing the unending pure love of this realm, you will have a beautiful earth life filled with joy and happiness, and this is what each soul hopes to be able to do before going down to earth.

When you flow clear/pure, love you raise your frequency... the vibration of your particles... to a level that is closer to this realm. Since this is your true/eternal home and your true essence/frequency, the closer you are to these things, the better you feel. As your frequency gets closer and closer to this realm, your life becomes more and more joyful.

All is love; however, on earth love exists in something you could describe as varying "strengths" or dilutions. If you think of love as the light that you know it is, you can understand this because you know that different lights have differing qualities. They can be more or less bright or 'pure'. This variability in light also exists in love. There are differing strengths or purity levels in the love itself. On top of that, there are differing quantities of love flowing through each being in each moment.

Here, we are fully flowing pure love and it flows as/on/with/via light, but on earth, you generally flow less pure love and you tend to flow it in lesser quantities. Always, though, each of you has a choice in determining for yourself the "dilution" level of the love you flow outward and how much love you choose to flow.

Love can flow into and through and out of you whenever you choose that in any aspect of your day-to-day living on earth:

in how you are being, what you are thinking, and what you are doing.

Imagine that as you are teaching, you freely choose to teach with passion, patience and caring. In this scenario, the passion, the patience and the caring that you are flowing outward from yourself to your students flow outward from you as clear, pure forms of love. You know you are doing all you can to help these students learn and grow, and you are doing it because you want to. When you teach in this way, you are flowing a high-quality love and you are sending it forth in large quantities. As you do this, you feel very happy —even buoyant. The reason you feel so wonderful is that by flowing out an undiluted, high-quality love, you are choosing something that brings the vibrational frequency of *earthly* you closer to this heaven realm and closer to the vibration of your essence: pure love.

If you are teaching, however, and you choose to teach with anger toward the students and perhaps resentment of the school administration (or anyone or anything else at all), this will not feel good because you will not be flowing clear and pure love during the action of teaching. Instead you will be flowing out a much less clear, less loving, less pure version of energy in the form of anger and resentment. You are still flowing, but what you are flowing is not very close to your essence, so this method of teaching will move your frequency further from that of heaven and all that you IN ESSENCE are.

Your lives on earth are made up of individual moments, and in each and every moment there are all kinds of different options for the quality and quantity of love you choose to flow.

The specific actions you choose during your life on earth are not nearly as important as the quality and quantities of love that you choose to flow in each moment. If you want to feel like you are in heaven while on earth, flow the purest love you can in the highest quantities you can-- while being, thinking about, and doing whatever things you choose.

If you are *not feeling good*, it is because you are *not flowing* pure/strong/unmuddied love often enough or in great enough quantities. If you are consistently *feeling good*, you are flowing *fairly clear love* in *decent quantities*. If you are consistently feeling *great*, it is because you are consistently flowing *very clear love* in *massive quantities*.

The formula is simple: the more clear/pure/ close-to-essence-quality love you flow, the better you feel. The more consistently you flow huge quantities of sparkling love outward, the more consistent your experience of joy will be.

Another way to say this is that it is not so much *what* you do but rather *HOW* you do what you do (and think) that determines how you feel. It is not the other way around as many on earth believe.

You have always loved teaching, Dear One. Like your father before you and his parents before him, you have always taught with passion, care, and patience and with the pure purpose of helping others to improve their lives. In doing so, you have taught with a clean, pure love flowing outward from you in massive quantities to all of your students. In your working life, this has kept your vibrational frequency high and close to heaven/your essence. Your working life has, therefore, been extremely joyful.

But your feelings of unworthiness and deep-seated hate for yourself have meant you have also sent very diluted/muddy love to yourself in massive quantities. By doing this, you have pulled your vibration down in most life areas outside of your work life.

For these reasons, your life has been like a roller coaster going up and down and up and down and up and down emotionally. This way of "flowing" has resulted in you experiencing many very high HIGHS and many very low LOWS.

You have liked the variety of this in some ways: you found the huge variation between the highs and the lows exciting. However, at some points your lows have been so low that you have considered suicide.

There is a more joyful way to live with variety on earth. You can find variety through choosing different types of things or situations to flow pure love to. This variety in situations will keep you intrigued, and this way of living will lead to a more joyful life overall because you will eliminate the lows without taking away the highs.

Some opt to flow ever muddier and muddier energy outward over the course of their time on earth. The lower the vibrational frequency of the energy being flowed, the less love there is in it (and vice versa). The less love that is being flowed, the less joyful the earth life will be.

To get to THIS place, to get to heaven, you have to choose pure love, and each of you always has a choice about what to choose.

All will *ultimately* choose love because love is all that really exists, but at present many on earth are living lives from perspectives that do not allow them to see this larger truth, and so many are not choosing the purest love available to them.

When you are in heaven before you go to earth, you always hope that while on earth you will be able to remember that you continue to be love (made of love) even while you are in a physical body, and even when the challenges seem huge.

When you hold this perspective and live sending out from yourself high-quality love in spite of the challenges you have chosen, your soul feels the success of the mountain climber who reaches the top of the mountain. The bigger the challenge your soul chooses for the life on earth, the higher the mountain you are choosing to climb in your life on earth. People with bigger challenges chose those because they wanted to climb bigger mountains.

In each moment of your existence you have a choice to choose to flow clear love fully and give it joyfully or not. The more you flow this loveliest love freely, the lighter you will be (the higher the frequency of your vibration will be) and the closer to heaven you will be while on earth. The more you flow love in this way, the better you will feel because your true/pure essence IS this high vibration of heaven, and it feels good to be moving closer and closer to your essence/heaven.

While you feel better and better as you move closer to your essence, the opposite is also true. If move further and further from your essence, you feel worse and worse. Going back and forth (pure love faucet on, pure love faucet off) creates the emotional roller-coaster scenario that you, Dear Leslie, know all too well.

Some of you pick really big challenges that might even tempt you to want to hate instead of loving. If anyone is dealing with a huge challenge that he/she has had for a very long time, it is likely there because that being's essence chose that challenge and the whole family (before going to earth) agreed to the scenario to allow you to take this thing on. There are no mistakes.

Do not worry about other's challenges or apparent lack of them. You cannot know what another soul's objective was before going to earth.

Look only at your own challenge and aim to see it as an opportunity to live in love especially when that is not easy to do.

If you have given yourself a more difficult life challenge, it is because your soul wanted that and felt ready for it before leaving heaven. Pat yourself on the back and move forward in love. Love is always the answer. Always.

By the way, those who decide to take on big challenges on earth are seen as big adventurers by ALL in the light, and there are more beings than you can imagine cheering for you to choose love. We all know it will take immense courage to live flowing love --due to the difficulty level of the chosen challenge-- while on earth. All who are looking at you from heaven's perspective know that you have before you an amazing opportunity to experience love, light, and life in new and different configurations and to act with and from purest possible love in all circumstances. We are cheering for you. You are never alone.

I absorbed all of this.

...And GODLIGHT continued to hold me and shine knowledge into me in the form of light. He was teaching me with love. My heart was smiling. I was warm and joyful --snuggled in the cocoon of GODLIGHT's love.

Chapter 15

Folded up

Sometimes when I put on a freshly-laundered pair of jeans, I feel a piece of paper in one of the pockets. I know even before I touch the paper and pull it out that this piece of paper will be all folded up. Since the jeans just came from the washing machine, I know this paper has gone through the wash as well. I love the feeling of knowing a surprise is ahead when I feel that piece of "something" in my pocket.

Sometimes it's a five dollar bill! (Yee-haw!! Unexpected money!!)

Sometimes it's a note I've written to myself, or sometimes it's a business card. There are lots of things it could be.

Imagine that going through the wash is like a dimensional shift. When you take those papers out of your pockets, sometimes you can read everything that was on the paper before, and sometimes there is some information that has been lost by going through the wash (that dimensional shift).

If it is a business card or a receipt or anything professionally printed, it often stays pretty much intact. But if it is something handwritten, especially if it was written in ink, some or much- or possibly *all*- of the message could have been blurred or washed away in the wash. Perhaps the paper itself has even begun to disintegrate.

But you (or at least I) don't really even remember what that paper originally was or why it's even **in** my pocket, until I notice it in my jeans, take it out of that pocket, and unfold it (or examine the remains of whatever it *was*).

In much the same way, when I got back to earth, while I had a clear memory of all the events that I had experienced in heaven, a lot of the *knowledge* that had been transferred to me was like pieces of paper in my jeans that had gone through the wash.

This was particularly true of the middle part of the discussion with GODLIGHT. The beginning and the end pieces of it were very clear in my mind from the moment I was back in my body... but the middle? It got stuck in my jeans and had a difficult trip through the dimensional shift.

The knowledge from the middle section of that conversation was a bit of an enigma when I first got back. I knew I had been told many wonderfully amazing things, and I somehow *felt* the knowledge that was with me, but I didn't have conscious knowledge of it or know how to access it.

The messages were with me like those folded up pieces of paper, but instead of being in my jeans, these packets of information were with me in the pockets of my heart and mind and even in my very cells... and I felt them there. I felt them in the same way that you feel that paper in the pockets of your jeans. But I couldn't figure out how to get them out of my pockets.

Even when I did figure out how to get to the messages, everything was still all folded up, and I needed to open the messages up individually. This took time.

Additionally, a few of the messages didn't fare so well in the wash. With these, I was generally only able to get a few words of the original message. A couple messages even disintegrated so that no part of the message was retrievable. But these were the minority by far.

Today, I am blissful about the fact that the large majority of the messages were still in great shape even *after* my dimensional shift—once I finally got access to them back on earth.

But there in the moment with GODLIGHT, everything was perfect. Warm and wonderful, the knowledge flowed into me as light, and I had access to everything and understood everything completely. Every one of my questions was answered at the moment it was formulated.

I flowed out questions to the loving-est LIGHT as it held me, and the answers came into me like the most magnificent morning sun on your skin. When I opened theses messages from the middle part of the discussion up later, back on earth, they still felt equally amazing.

Joy. Truth. Love. Heaven. ...All on earth.

Chapter 16

Sparklers and Fireworks

The messages GODLIGHT shared with me as he held me were understood by me perfectly in the moment I received them because at that moment I was in my essence form: existing as pure love.

However, when I got back to earth, although I clearly remembered being held and receiving huge quantities of information from GODLIGHT during this part of my visit to heaven, the messages themselves were not accessible to me initially because of the huge contrast between Leslie in the realm of light and Leslie on earth. I felt the light and love of the messages, but I could not access the actual content.

It was only when I had flowed love sufficiently to become closer to my essence and the essence of heaven that I was able to open these messages, "read" them, and then put them into earthly language in order to share them.

Each time I gained access to a new message, it felt like a celebration. Each and every one of these messages opened inside as well as before and above me. I felt their light/love and saw the messages when I was high enough vibrationally to do so.

I have put the words from GODLIGHT in this chapter all into italics. Before each new message, I have placed an asterisk as a reminder of the light that the messages arrived on.

The shorter ones danced (gleefully!!) when they expressed themselves to me as white light. Much like sparklers on Independence Day, their light was captivating. Yet, unlike traditional sparklers, these messages were somehow alive. They were much more than just dancing light. These contained love and truth-- and it felt to me as if the light, in addition to being a conscious loving message, was a mode of transportation for the messages as well.

The larger messages that follow each felt to me like bursts of breath-taking white fireworks of love and truth. Though they were far quieter than earthly fireworks, their messages glittered in my heart with a beauty beyond description. The glory of this light that is love combined with the beauty of the truths being given to me --creating a fireworks display unparalleled on earth.

In addition to the messages themselves touching me, the love and beauty of the **way** in which these messages were communicated to me resulted in each new message feeling as if it were the best present I had ever received.

It is my grandest wish that every reader might experience these messages in this way as well; because it is the closest I can get in earthly terms to describing how these felt to me as they entered my heart, and it is in that same loving spirit that I desire to share them.

And so, I invite you to imagine that you are seated outside in a place you love. It is evening and a perfect temperature. You are comfortable and content in every way. You are breathing deeply and your heart is fully open. You have a wonderful feeling that you are about to experience something amazing. And then trumpets blast!! ...And you know the sparklers and fireworks show from Godlight is about to begin.

The first sparkling messages flow in on light slowly.

You are made of love.   (The words sparkle their way directly into your heart.)

You are eternal. (More sparkling --and it continues this way...!!)

This (the realm of light) is your true home. This home is eternal.

This home is always changing. We are currently expanding.

The fabric of the universe is love. Love in heaven is seen as light.

These messages are reminders to you of things that the eternal part of you already knows to be true, and for this reason, you will feel a wonderful resonance with these messages.

*You are comprised of, made **of,** this universal fabric of love. You are literally OF this love. You, and all, are created from the essence of love and it is how it is such that **all** are comprised of love.*

*ALL that exists, all that is, **is** love. Love --and all-- comes from the **ALL,** and it is that **ALL** that is sending you these messages now.

*You came from here, this realm of light. You left here to go to the earth dimension.

*All that are on the earth originated here.

*All now living on earth **chose** to go to the dimension of earth.

AND NOW THE FIREWORKS JOIN IN—OPENING ABOVE YOU IN WHITE LIGHT AND POURING INTO YOUR HAPPY HEART...

*Your time on earth is a short period of time away from this, your eternal home. You understand it is so when you go to earth. You know the time out of this dimension will be very short compared to all of eternity which you will have in heaven.

*Just as your true home is heaven, your true form of communication is not language as it is used on earth at present.

*Traditional earth languages have been used by people in bodies because their frequencies previously were not high enough (as a general population) to interact in the way we do here in heaven.

*Here in heaven, you know we speak in a language of love/light and that we send our thoughts to one another through this medium of love/light as I am doing with you now. This is a more direct method of communicating than exists in the languages of the earth because this is communication through essence. This method of communication is a perfect fit for heaven because all in heaven is/are in essence form (pure and light with a high frequency vibration of their particles).

*You have noticed that the frequency of your vibrating particles here is at a much higher/faster rate than when you were previously in a body on earth. You have noticed that all and ALL here vibrate at this faster rate. The form of communication that we use here in heaven is the norm for those at this frequency. It is only "picked up" by those in lower realms who have sufficiently high frequencies to "catch" our messages.

*For many, many years there have been people on earth who have been considered to be psychics or mediums. These people have said that they are able to communicate with "the other side". In fact, those people have been communicating with other realms by changing their frequency to "match" the frequency of other realms.

*The frequency on earth today is (overall) much lower than in heaven, but there are individuals on earth with frequencies quite close to that of their essence/the essence of heaven. There are others on earth who are far below even the average, low vibration of earth's frequency.

*Realms exist below the current earth frequency as well as above it. Heaven, this realm, is above the earth frequency.

*Those on earth who flow clear love openly and fully most of the time-- and through doing so raise their frequency to the point where they are consistently high enough to be able to communicate in this form of heavenly communication-- will become more and more common on earth in the near future (as time is perceived on earth). However, this multi-dimensional communication has been happening for eons.

*Dear One, let the people of earth know that they can ALL talk with heaven if only they choose to flow purest love in each moment; if they choose to live such that the frequency of their vibration on earth is closer to heaven.

*Heaven is sending out messages to earth all the time, but few are they who currently receive these messages.

*Additionally, living on earth simply **feels** better when your particles are vibrating at a frequency that is closer to heaven, and this is because the heaven state is your natural state. It is the state of your essence. When on earth, the closer you live to this state, the better you will feel AND the more you will be attuned to the communications being sent to you on/in/via the light that is that love which is the love of ALL.

*Each human on earth has a "heaven team". To speak to your heaven team from earth, you only need to maintain a state in which you are as high/light/full of love as possible. From that place, you will hear the communications which are coming to you on earth from your heaven team. These types of heavenly communications are going out to all on earth, but most are not able to hear them at present.

*Your heaven team's goal is always to help you live in love on earth and to follow your soul's personal interests while on earth.

*You will see your heaven team soon, Dear One... After we finish this discussion.

*The way we communicate in heaven is more natural and easy for you than speaking earth languages. This form of communication is flowing into you on light and that light is love. I send the message and the love/light to you simultaneously and you are responding to me in the same way. You know how to do this without needing to be taught. It happens easily when the frequency is love-filled.

*How is it that you know how to communicate this way? It is because this communication form is merely love flowing. And because you are love and all is love, and because it is a natural aspect of love for it to flow, it is natural that we flow our love to one another and share all that we know and are-- for we are all love and, therefore, we are –in the truest sense- all actually one and the same. And so it is that it is natural and normal for you and for all to communicate this way during the time you are in heaven before you go to earth. This is so because it is a natural part of who you truly are.

*Now... most in bodies on earth at the present time have chosen to go to earth more than once previously. It is always your choice to go or stay here in the light. You always know you will return here eventually before you go, so going out from heaven for an adventure is a fun choice. But it is always a choice.

You wiggle deeper into your seat as a few more sparklers of loving messages appear in the air before you:

Love is light.

I love you.

* *I love all. Each of you is the all and also yourself.*

I love you/all... More than you can imagine. (Your heart swells with joy now, knowing this to be true.)

You are strong. Stronger than you know.

You are beautiful. More beautiful than you know.

*You are **amazing**- just by virtue of your existence- for you are a cell of GOD.*

Each living thing on earth is a cell of my essence.

I love each part of each part. This is true whether you remember it or not.

You chose to go to earth with what you have called the abyss, the void, the problem. You chose it for a reason. But it does not mean you are less than all that you are.

You are a piece of GODLIGHT now and forever.

I am the ALL. The ALL is LOVE.

*All things breathe in one way or another.

* For love, the method of "breathing" is flowing. It flows as light. LOVE must flow. It must move in order to live.

*Love is light and light is love. It can be particle or it can flow, but it is always both.

*There is much happening on earth that most are unaware of. Just as a dog hears sounds that a human cannot hear, it does not mean the sounds are not there. In this same way, there is light that most of you on earth cannot see—yet it exists. The light of which I speak is love flowing in the form of messages from heaven and from those on earth with a vibrational frequency near that of heaven.

*Because you are made of love, and because love needs to flow in order for it to "breathe" and live, **you** need to flow love in order to flourish. And so, flowing love is, in sum, the key to life.

*It is also the way to be nearest heaven while on earth.

*You will go back to earth and you will flow love and you will tell others of this truth. You will be a flow-er: a flower of love and light.

*Everything in the natural world is made of love. Any other knowing is not a true knowing, just as your belief about your defect was not a true knowing. If a belief does not flow love, it is not an eternal truth.

*This is your True Home.

*This is everyone's True Home.

*All come from here and all will eventually return here.

...NOW YOU ARE FEELING EXHILARATED, AND LARGER MESSAGES ARE OPENING ALL AROUND YOU SO THAT THE SKY FILLS WITH THEIR LIGHT:

*You had/have some things you wanted/want to do that you cannot do in heaven because of the way the heaven dimension is configured. Here we do not have time and space and physicality and separateness in the way they exist on earth.

*As you have noted, here in the realm of light there is really no difference between the moment I say a thing and the moment you know the thing or between the knowing/thinking of the thing and the experience of the thing itself.

*Thought and creation happen in the same instant here which is why you are becoming all that I am saying even as I say it. You do not need to process it in the way you would on earth.

128

You know it AND become it AS I say it. (In fact, you were actually it before I said it but did not remember it so you did not know that part of yourself.) This instantaneous-ness is a part of the realm of light in which we now are.

Things do not play out in this "instantaneous" way outside of the realm of light. In the earth dimension, BE-ing has different rules of play. Because the rules are different, it feels like a different game. But it is all a part of the larger game of life.

There are games within games within games. (This particular message hangs before you for a very long time. You continue to ponder it even as other, different messages shine into your heart.)

*The entire universe is breathing. Heaven is breathing. Earth is breathing. Down to the cellular level and even lower. Everything is blinking on and off, or in and out, or up and down, or dark and light. It is all moving in order to be breathing. Every last bit of it. This **is** life.*

This is why everything is always changing. The change is a form of "breathing". This constant change is why in each and every moment you have a choice. It is because things change in each moment. And in each moment, therefore, you have the choice to choose the thing is that is closest to heaven (LOVE/LIGHT) – or to choose a different thing. And no matter how many choices you think you have, there are always more choices, and more and more and more.

*The more you flow love and light, the closer to heaven you will be. From a higher position, you will see more and be aware of more choices for your life. Everyone sees different choices depending upon how close to or far from heaven they are in any given moment, and this is directly related to the quality and quantity of love being flowed by that person in any moment.

*It is in the choices and movement that life is expressed and lives. Life itself must breathe. Love must flow in order to live. And so you go to earth to live: to play; to learn; to enjoy; to breathe in and out in new and different ways.

Why do you think it was so wonderful for you to expand and contract yourself when you were playing/exploring here earlier? It is for the same reason that if a person places his hand on your hand and then does not move it for a long period of time, you will forget that the hand is there. It is because **it is in the movement that the thing is known.*

*THIS is the game: movement and change. Life is energy moving, love flowing. At the heart of it is how you choose to flow, to BE in each moment.

*You go to earth when you choose to go to earth, and you choose to go to earth because there are things you want to experience on earth that you cannot experience here.

*Here there is no becoming. To be in the process of "becoming" is to be in the process of moving from being one thing to being a different thing. The act of "being in the process" takes time. Here... there is no time in this sense because in the moment a thing is thought, it simply IS. And so in heaven, there is no becoming. There is only thought and being and they are one and the same with no separation.

*Earth is a realm for playing with separation.

*You opt to go to the earth realm of separation partly as a way to feel the shifting from one state to the next. Here we are one. There you feel as if you are separate. You are still one, but you feel as if you are separate because that is a part of the way the earth dimension is configured. This movement from heaven to earth in itself creates a contrast which is fun for souls to experience.

*When you go to earth, you switch between the state of knowing you are ALL (here) and forgetting you are ALL (there). This knowing/forgetting rhythm forms a breathing pattern of its own.

131

*As I have said before: all living things breathe in one way or another. This is so from the level of the macro to the level of the micro.

*Even the universe itself breathes. It expands over billions of your earth years and then contracts over billions of years, and then expands and then contracts again and again and again. This is life. This is the movement. This is the universe breathing.

*You each know and understand all of this as you choose to go down to earth. You want to feel the separation temporarily (in order to feel the hand moving so to speak) and you agree to "forget" aspects of who you truly are in order to have the full experience.

*It is the change we desire. It is the hand moving that we all appreciate. Out and in, out and in, out and in. Down to earth, and up to heaven, and down to earth and up to heaven. Into the darkness, into the light, into the darkness and into the light.

The big fireworks fade out slowly and new sparklers joyfully join in:

*All of these are forms of change.

*But in any form always **all** parts are a part of the **ALL**--even if they have forgotten this truth.

*Just because the darkness has forgotten it came from the light does not mean that it is not of the light.

*Coming back to the light is a choice. It is something anyone can do if he so chooses.

*This place is your true home because it is where you come from—where all living things originate-- and so we wait here for you to come back after you finish the goals you set out to accomplish when you left.

*Yes. You went forth with an aim in addition to breathing. You wanted to experience and do certain things.

*There is no "right" or "wrong" as they are often defined on earth. However it is truth that your choices will take you to a lighter/higher vibrational place or to a less light place. Choosing the lightest choice from among the options you are aware of is always going to feel better than the less light choice because the lighter the choice, the closer it is to your essence which is love (which is the light that you see in heaven).

*All are of GOD/ALL and all are of equal value. You are not more "worthy" or less "worthy" than any other. You are all beautiful and valuable by your existence itself. You do not need to **do** anything to earn or gain value.

*Your essence is the essence of heaven because you and all come from here and it is for this reason that when you choose light you feel better—because you resonate with that which is a match to your own essence. When any of you on earth chooses to live at a vibrational place that is as close as you can get to that of your heavenly essence while on earth, through living in this love-filled way you will be so close to the vibration of heaven that you will have access to the glory of the heaven realm—even while on earth.

*Therefore, we would gently remind you that while there is no right or wrong, when you are in doubt about what to do in any situation, if you choose love, you will always feel better. This is so because you ARE love and by choosing this path you will come closer to your essence. When you act from love, in addition to feeling better, you will also see more and better options (from the higher/lighter vantage point), have access to your heaven team, and live a more joyful life.

* Love is the path of light. Light brings you closer to heaven. You will feel lighter and be lifted to a higher place where you will see more and better options as you become more light-filled on earth.

*Get lighter by flowing more light. Flow more light by doing what I have shown you here.

*Live to give love. Live to flow light. Living is loving. Loving is living. This is the path of light. This is the path to True Home.

*When you live flowing love, life is joyful.

*You can "lift" the way you feel in any moment by sending the purest possible light/love outward from yourself. You can send it back to yourself, and to beings and events in your past, present, or future. But the present is the only moment from which you can make such a choice, and the present is truly all that exists in any dimension at any given moment. This is because a new universe exists in each new moment, with each new breath. We, too, are blinking on and off and with each blinking back on, we are more and new and different --even if it does not appear to be so.

*The present is the moment that is alive in this sense. It is the only moment in which you can either be flowing love or not flowing love.

*It does not matter where you flow love or whom you flow love to. What matters is that you choose to flow love in each moment of the present- if you desire to live a joyful life and resonate with heaven.

*Appreciating is a form of flowing love on earth. Flowing appreciation to everyone and everything is to live in heaven while on earth. Giving in this way is a heavenly act.

*When you flow love in this way, either directly (as light/love) or indirectly (in the form of time, money, help, friendship, etc.) to others, you will be refilled with love. This is so by design.

* This is so because when you give all of the light that is inside you away joyfully, this type of joyful giving creates a kind of vacuum in your earth body/vessel. Your body is an amazing vessel in this way: the vacuum created within you by giving from your heart/soul in this loving manner actually acts **as** a vacuum acts. It pulls more love from heaven into you--into the vacuum within you. In this way, the more you give, the more you get. This is why the way to have more of anything is to give it away joyfully while knowing that heaven will give you a "free refill".

*And so, the more you give in this joyful way, the more of all that you have given will come back to you. However, this heavenly vacuum the pulls in more love is **only** created when the form of giving is a giving in which there is no expectation of anything in return—when the giving is from a place of pure love/light/joy. The giver in this scenario finds joy in the flowing outward itself which the giving **is**. This form of giving is the flowing of love—this **is** the living.

*Because we are all made of heavenly love, and because love needs to "breathe" (as I have described already) in order to fully live, there are negative consequences to not flowing love. You see, love "breathes" through flowing, and love is flowed in the way just explained. If you do not breathe in this heavenly way while on earth, your earth vessel cannot be all it was designed to be.

*Now, the light/love that comes into your body when you create this vacuum may flow into your vessel in the form of love or health or joy or wealth. All of these are forms of light. All of these are love. All of these are truth coming to you from the realm of light-- heaven—where all love originates.

*When you live this way, light flows through you. It comes in from heaven and goes out through the heart.

*The more you flow love out, the more quickly you create a vacuum in your body, and the more quickly your vessel will be refilled with light from heaven. And then you will have more love to flow out once more, and the cycle repeats again and again and again.

*When we live flowing love in this way, there is so much light flowing through us that we may even appear to others to be radiating light.

*Many times, beings who live or have lived in this way have had so much light flowing into and out of them, that they are described as having a halo. This halo effect is the result of the huge quantities of light flowing from heaven into the body where the vacuum is created. The more a person flows love in this way, the more radiant the person becomes.

... NOW TRUMPETS BLAST ONCE MORE--SIGNALING THE GRAND FINALE AS MESSAGES EXPLODE *ABOVE AND BEFORE YOU EVERYWHERE IN LIGHT AND JOY...*

*You/all go there (earth) knowing of this realm. But the knowing is "buried". This is part of the configuration of being on earth.

*In this way, you all agree to a certain form of amnesia when you go down there, but you all also get to pick certain gifts to take. When you leave here, you hope the gifts you take to the realm of separation will jog your memory to help you remember the way things truly are.

*And so, down you go...into individual bodies on earth. These bodies make you feel separate (although as you know from being here, we are truly all one).

*And you experience separation in time. There is the time between the thinking of the thing and the becoming of the thing. There is also the feeling of past, present and future

138

which exist in a very different sense in this realm. (The remainder of this message did not make it through the dimensional shift.)

* Additionally, there is space-- which adds to the feeling of being separate. Each space feels different and separate, and when you are in a body, you must move your physical body (or the body needs to be moved) through space to get to another space.

*As we/I said before, here (in heaven) in the moment a thought is expressed, it simply IS. The creation process is the same in the earth realm except that on earth there is the experience of a time delay between the thought and the coming into existence of the thought. There is actually NO time delay...because there is actually no such thing as time, but in a dimension where it feels like there is time, it will also feel like there is a separation between a thought and that thought coming into being.

*These forms of separation feel very real to you while on earth.

*The delay in "becoming" on earth can be envisioned by thinking of the difference between digital cameras and film cameras.

*When you take a picture with a digital camera, you see the image immediately. When you take a photo with a camera that is using film, you need to develop the film before you can see the images. But in both camera types, the image is made in the instant the photo is taken. It is so with your desires in heaven and on earth.

*Your life on earth is like the camera that uses film. When you wish for a thing, it is like you take a photo. Then you have to wait for the photo to be developed to see the photo (because you are in a realm of separation). In the same way there is separation between what you desire on earth and what you see as your creation.

*Because of the separation in time between the thought and the experience of the creation, many on earth do not understand that their thoughts are creating the experience. However, in the instant you take the photo -whether the camera is digital or uses film--the photo itself already **exists.**

*In the same way, in the instant that you desire something, the answer to that desire also exists.

*Just because the photo has not been developed in your experience in the earth dimension does **not** mean it does not yet exist. It exists in the moment you take the photo: it is only that it has not yet been developed from the perspective of the being on earth. In the same way, you create in the instant you have a desire, but there is a separation in time between asking for a thing and seeing that thing.

Many times, while you are on the way to "get your film developed", you on earth drop the undeveloped film – your dreams and ideas—into the trash because you do not understand the way the process works. You often make the mistake of thinking there is nothing on the film when that is not the case at all.

*The way to develop your "film" on earth (experience the things you dream of) is to know and live knowing that the picture already exists once you take a photo—even if it has not yet been developed.

*Both realms have cameras. Both realms have the same ability to take photos and have them exist immediately. But on earth – because of the separation in time between taking the photo and getting it developed— many of you do not understand the actual relationship that exists between your thoughts and your experiences in your life.

*There is a never-ending supply of love and all things are made of love. Because of this, there is enough of everything for all to have whatever they/we/you desire.

*This universe and everything in it exists for your exploration, and you and all beings have equal rights to explore every bit of it. This is not a problem because the fountain from which all comes is infinite. Because of this, there is enough for everyone to have all that they desire. I am infinite, and so no desire is too big for me to answer. The idea of "not enough" is a false truth. Anything that does not bring you closer to heaven's light is a false truth.

Earth is your playground, created for you to play in and take pictures and experience separateness and live and flow love.

*Life is joyful when you live this way—flowing light and love to one and all in all ways, always.

*You go to earth because you want to play the game with different "settings" than those that you have here. Here you think it and you are it. They are overlaid one upon the other and one cannot exist without the other. There... it is not so. And this is by design.

*Now, some of you choose to go to earth more as what you might call "collectives" with more of what could be termed a group mission.

*Those who "die" en masse in plagues, genocides, etc. have often chosen this as a collective mission before going to earth.

Of course, there is no "death" in the way many imagine it to be from the earth dimension because your essence is eternal.

Others go to earth as individuals with more of what could be termed **individual aspirations.*

*We/You choose your families with members heading down one by one... each one a few earth years before or after the other. All of this is by design so that the plan (whatever your plan was while here in heaven) will unfold as you/we/ALL chose to have it unfold.

*In all things, you have a choice. If you always desire to choose the most light-filled choice, your heart/essence will move toward love and live in love. Sadness only exists when you forget you are light/one/love/all and when you forget the truth.

*If you feel sad, review these messages and remember all that you are. Even when you do not remember us, we remember and love you. If you feel sad, look for things in your life that are going well. Flowing love as thanks for even the smallest of things going well in your life will shift your path. Give thanks for these small things—whatever they may be. In this way, work your way back toward flowing love more than not flowing love, and your sadness will be gone.

*What flows toward you is determined by the quality and quantity of love you flow outward—but for it to flow INTO you, your vessel must be open to receiving from heaven.

*If your vessel is closed to receiving, even if you DO create the vacuum, you will not receive these gifts which are meant for you because the clogged opening to your vacuum will prohibit these gifts from entering.

*To have your heavenly dreams come true on earth, KNOW that you are a cell in the being that is God/ALL THAT IS and that you are as VALUABLE and DESERVING of ALL as ALL THAT IS because you are a particle of ME: you are a part of the whole. Living with this knowing will keep your vessel open for receiving from the universe.

*KNOW that your giving and flowing love in conjunction with your knowledge of your true identity will bring you closer to the light and it will make your most beautiful 'photos' develop more quickly.

*KNOW all that you are. Look at the sky, and know that it is you --and you are it.

*Anything is possible if you choose to live this way.

Chapter 17

Treasure Chests

GODLIGHT lovingly shared enough information to fill all the libraries on earth.

After GODLIGHT shared all of these wonderful truths with me, I was still in his arms. I have remembered all along how our time together in heaven ended.

Godlight and I went on to discuss in great depth and detail the specific things I had wanted to do when I had originally gone down to earth as Leslie. These things, GODLIGHT explained to me, were things that I had not yet completed at the time of my trip to heaven. He said that Leslie on earth had not yet consciously learned what her soul had wanted to do on earth.

When I was later back in my body, although I knew we discussed this topic at great length, I could not remember the details of my soul's full wanting which GODLIGHT and I discussed as he held me.

I believe this is so because this is part of the agreement we each sign on to when we decide to come to earth. In a way, the time on earth is like a treasure hunt and the specific things each of our souls wanted to accomplish while in heaven are buried like treasure somewhere in the earth dimension. We come down here to earth and are excited to begin the hunt for our soul's treasure chest.

To find the treasure chest (with our soul's grandest desires inside) we only need to follow the path of joy on earth. If we live in love and light and follow the path our essence tells us feels best, we can discover anew in the earth dimension what our specific intentions from heaven were, and we will each find our very own treasure chest which holds the KNOWING of the desires we each have in heaven.

Once I understood this, GODLIGHT flowed to me a message which formally closed the time of our discussion.

GO FORTH NOW AND LIVE IN LIGHT UPON THE EARTH.

Chapter 18

Free Will

I am not proud of this next part of the story, but since it happened I am including it here. When GOD expressing himself as most-magnificent LIGHT finished sharing all of this magnificence with me, can you guess what I did?

Did I happily agree to leave the light to return to earth and hunt treasure?

Oh, no. Not by a long shot.

I was not nearly that strong, brave, or mature.

While it is completely humiliating to admit this, the fact is that I...well, I threw a complete, full-on tantrum in front of GODLIGHT…. because I didn't want to leave heaven.

Like a two-year-old child who doesn't like what he's just been told, I burst into the non-physical equivalent of a conniption fit. I cried and I wailed. I begged and I pleaded, and then I cried some more. (*Very* embarrassing to admit, but it's exactly what I did.)

As I did this, I felt GODLIGHT's light smiling upon me, and the love he was flowing to me felt as if it was actually turned *up* a notch (!!!!) and he continued to hold me and send me love until I eventually calmed down.

It was a very good lesson for me. If people around me now do things that stem from a dark/fearful place, I follow GODLIGHT's example and just calmly turn up the volume on the love I'm flowing out to them.

Once I was calm, he gently reminded me again of all the things we had already discussed including what I had set forth to do in the body of Leslie on earth-- which I had not yet accomplished. He also reminded me yet again about living in light and love on earth.

But I was adamant. I loved being in the light, and I did not want to go back to earth. Earth made me feel sad.

GODLIGHT then told me that I actually had a choice, and that I *could* stay in the Realm of Light instead of going back to earth--if that was what I truly wanted to do.

He would not force me to go back. He told me that we all always have choices and in this it was no different.

He explained that each soul not only decides when it wants go *to* earth but that each soul also chooses when it wants to leave the body at the end of the life on earth. This is true for every soul. Each being leaves earth when and **only when** the

148

soul of that being is ready to go. This choice does not come from the body. The choice to leave earth is a choice from the essence of the being, from the soul.

From within the earth when things play out, the things we experience may seem to us or to our earth family and friends like tragedies. If a child has died on earth or when a loved one has unexpectedly been killed in a tragic way, it may seem from the earth perspective that these things are tragedies. However, they are not tragedies from the level of heaven. There is no death as it is understood on earth, and there are no tragedies.

These choices are a part of what those essences chose to experience for reasons that may be known on the earth plane only to that one soul. From the earth dimension it may be hard to see the larger picture of what is happening, but no one dies on earth except when their soul is ready to make the change out of the earth realm.

And now, here I was being given that choice: to "die" or not; to stay in heaven or return to earth. While the choice was mine, it was very, **very** clear that GODLIGHT had a definite opinion about what he wanted me to choose.

He really thought going back to earth was the best thing for me because he knew there were things I had wanted to do that I had not yet accomplished. Even so, he still gave me the final say in the matter, because (as he explained) it is my life and it is not his decision to make. So, I was given the opportunity to choose whatever I wanted. Even though it was clear that GODLIGHT wanted me to return to earth, I had free will to choose.

This knowledge has had a huge impact on me since returning to earth. I know that while GOD cares very deeply about what each of us decides to do, we always get to choose for ourselves what we are actually *going* to do. GOD does not step in and force us to do specific things with our lives.

We know what feels right to our essence (that choice which is the highest/lightest/purest), but we are free to live however we choose, and we can choose whatever we want. *And* we live with the results of our choices.

Whether you love to sing, play ball, paint, fix cars, be with animals, dance, ride motorcycles, or anything else...all of these are heavenly states of being on earth if you are flowing love while you are doing them.

GODLIGHT wanted me to know that the time we spend on earth is short compared to the time we spend in the realm of light. It is so short, in fact, that we can think of going to earth as something similar to going on a little weekend trip away from True Home. Since the time away from true home would be so short and since I would be doing things my soul wanted to do, I could go and feel joy about it. You don't get sad before you go on vacation because you know you will come home again. You can think of this in the same way.

He said, "You are a part of the whole and a part of the light, and you will do wonderful things if you go back because now you will live with heaven's perspective."

"Trust yourself, Dear One. You can and will be amazing. In fact, you already are. You always were-- as are all. Most just don't know it. But now you know. You are not better than another nor are you worse. You are simply amazing-- as are all."

God reminded me yet again that I was not defective and that there are no mistakes, he promised me that I would not be alone ever again (in fact I never had been alone, but I believed a false truth and that had led me to feel alone), and he explained that after I had done everything I needed to do, I would be able to return to heaven whenever it was that my soul made the decision to come back.

He reminded me again and again and again and again: LOVE. All is love. You are loved. Love is light. Spread light and love joyfully knowing that you are a part of heaven, and your life will be heaven on earth.

Chapter 19

My Heaven Team

It would be impossible not to trust this loving-est light, but even so, I *still* didn't want to leave heaven. I knew I was being stubborn, but when I thought of earth, I equated it with sadness and feeling alone. The place I was in was love, light, joy, peace, truth, freedom and unity all rolled into one. It seemed like the opposite of earth.

GODLIGHT continued to put me at ease about going back. He made it clear that from earth I would have all the knowledge I needed in order to "access" the feelings, knowledge, and thoughts of heaven—as well as any of my **friends** in heaven if I lived *as love and light* in the way I had been shown.

When he said this part about my friends, something exquisite happened! I had felt from the beginning that there -mixed into the light that I was in- were angels and people who loved me. I felt they comprised the light and were with me and had been with me since I'd arrived in the light. I had felt that all this time, but I had not *seen* any of them.

However, in the moment that GODLIGHT spoke of my friends, they were all there before me! They had indeed been there all along in the light but they had been there with *their particles* dispersed out into their extended versions so that they had been mingled into the whole, and I had not seen them as individuals but rather I had been experiencing them as the whole/the light of heaven itself.

Now, though, they had all simultaneously "condensed" down (as I had learned to playfully do earlier) so that they were all there near me in their "smaller" clustered/more compact states. They now appeared as individual essences of light within the larger light of the realm of light.

It was clear to me that they had moved into these individualized forms as a kind of present to me: so that I could see them as individuals instead of as the whole. Everyone I had ever known on earth and loved that had died was there and so were many others who I did not recognize the essences of immediately. From all of them I felt the love of family and friends. Whether I *recognized* them in their individualized light shapes or not, I knew that we all knew each other. I also knew they loved me deeply, and I felt a warm and deep love *for* them as well. I knew that I knew them all already somehow, and that I had, in fact, known them all for a long, long time. These were heaven relationships that continued when we were on earth, not the other way around.

Together we all comprised a *family* that included beings inside and outside of my earth family. This group was significantly larger than my earth family, and it was something like a "heaven team". Those who were gathered nearest me were the most *active/involved* members of my team. I understood that there in heaven we are all one, but this team is particularly close to me. I understood that many of these beings are active on *many* teams, and this is easy since when their particles go out and disperse, they can be in many places and doing many different things at once. The teams are grouped by soul interests, and a lot of the teams and team members overlap. So while you and your sister or brother are likely on each other's soul teams, each of them will have many on their teams that are not on your team and you will have beings on your team that on not on their teams. GODLIGHT is the only one who is on everyone's team. (I found that news particularly delightful!)

No team has all of its members on earth at the same time. This is by design.

One of those who was nearest me when the beings came into their condensed forms was my mom's mom. I felt the depth of her love for me and it was an incredibly joyful thing to feel her love flowing to me. I knew immediately it was her beautiful essence. She was herself, except that she looked nothing like she had on earth and was instead now a glowing, fluid body of light. Still I knew instantly it was her. I understood that it had been the essence of her that had loved me on earth and that that same essence was loving me now... indeed had always and would always love me.

It was here that I also first saw Archangel Gabriel who has since become my constant, beloved companion. Einstein, Leonardo DaVinci, and Walt Whitman are also on my heaven team. There were many, many others there speaking love to me in light language. Many of them told me they would be talking with me more when I was back on earth. They all made it clear that to talk with them from earth, all I needed to do was

safljasf;lsruoriuroiffvsfjs;lfkjsfsfjs;flks fjslfkjasr[w9evvnlkjasrljf sodivjw;rij;flksncs;hb[erfisj;fdv vwrwrjwfjas;wjafifjwfrr3ffjsfijflkcn;fhffjwf;lkjfawlfjwfwafwflwk jlfkj

and then

tbijbobnertboimglhmhlkgjd;gije tboiigvjegeg;kh;ljk;odooeiertfjffjglkgsdkfj!!

And when I did that, I would be able to communicate with them and in that way they would be back with me.

156

I write it the way I have above because that is how what they said to me felt when I first got back to earth. Their messages seemed/felt/WERE garbled. I knew that I KNEW how to decode the messages, but I didn't remember *how* and I couldn't ask them for help because I didn't know how to reach them since I couldn't decode their message about how to contact them from earth...

They continued saying they would continue to talk with me when I got back to earth and that they would answer any questions I asked if the questions were "of the light".

Then, in unison, as quickly as they had appeared in their condensed states, they all converted back to their expanded states. When they all shifted back to their expanded states, they became a part of the larger light again. But now I saw the light of heaven in a new way. "My team" had mingled back into the light, but now I knew them even while in their expanded states. I "saw" their individual particles now within the larger light as they shone love to me from all the ends of that realm. They were a part of the whole and also individuals, just as I knew myself to be, AND we were also a team! This knowing filled me anew to overflowing with joy. They were and are still—my eternal friends, my family in heaven, my heaven team.

Now that this had happened I *really* did not want to leave the realm of light, but it was pretty clear that they all felt I had things to be doing on earth, and I started to wonder if going back might actually be the best thing --even though I couldn't understand why or how that could be possible. I still really didn't fully understand *exactly* what I was supposed to be doing back on earth, and so I didn't feel equipped to go back yet.

GODLIGHT was still there larger than heaven itself and brighter than the combined "all of us" who had expanded back out into heaven, and he also promised me once again that I would come back here since this place was and always would be my home.

I knew God was telling me the truth, and everyone seemed really excited for me to have what they considered to be a great 'opportunity' to go back to earth. **They** all seemed to think I was ready for it.

With all this in my heart, I was nearly convinced. Once more I asked GODLIGHT to promise me that I would be able to return to heaven after my time on earth.

He/She/It/ALL/Love/Light/GODLIGHT, patient as ever, smiled love upon me and promised me yet again that I would come back. His patience and love in explaining this for the umpteenth time made me smile, and something moved within me.

I suddenly knew it would be ok... that in fact it would be better than ok. It would be wonderful to go back to earth.

I felt myself saying/sending a multi-layered message of love and light to GODLIGHT and all in heaven.

I said:

 I love you all/ALL. I choose to go back to earth.

The message went out as a single beam of love from me to all and ALL in that dimension.

And in that instant, I left heaven.

Chapter 20

Crash Landing

The trip back here began with all of my particles being crushed and crammed and smashed together-- combined with a sensation like the floor had fallen out from beneath me.

Ahhhhhhhhhhhhhhhh. Here we go..............

I wasn't completely surprised by this because I knew where I was going: from heaven back directly to the body I had seen on the table...back to my body on earth.

I *was* surprised by how quickly this happened and by the amount of force I felt.

From my expanded position of feeling that I was as big as the entire Realm of Light, my essence was squished and compressed all the way back to being able to fit into a human body. This happened with extreme speed.

This sensation of going from being expanded to being condensed...crushed down into a compacted version of what I had been just a moment before... felt very odd. When I had been in heaven, I had been willfully condensing myself. This situation very was different in that I was not the one controlling the condensing this time. It was now happening *to* me.

It was also different in that when I had been compacting my particles in heaven, I was compacting them into a very loose, hovering kind of cloud of light. The compression I had controlled had felt comfortable, relaxed, and easy. Now my particles were being forced much, much, much closer together. The compression did not hurt, but it was like being in a waaaaaaaaaaaay too crowded elevator. Comfortable would never be a word I would use to describe this.

While my particles were being "densified", I was also being pulled downward very rapidly. The pressure of this felt like being sucked downward into the biggest and strongest imaginable vacuum.

As I was being compressed, I was going down at the same time and was simultaneously also going from the lightness into the dark. I went from seeing and being a part of that huge expanse of light downward into a very long, ever darkening funnel-shaped place. It went downward into darkness. But I, Leslie, was not *separate* from the funnel I was in. I knew that it was my own contraction and movement downward that was forming the funnel itself.

If you held a huge book open above your head and then closed it while pulling it down rapidly, that would be a small-scale (less forceful) version of what I experienced. I was closing in on myself and going down, too.

As I went down, my non-physical head stayed in the upright position. I was not disoriented but I *did* feel myself losing my understanding of huge quantities of information that had, just a moment before, been so perfectly clear to me. I felt I was losing my comprehension of all the answers that had been so wonderful, simple, perfect, and beautiful.

I got smaller and smaller and more and more compressed as I continued down this funnel of me-ness **very** rapidly being sucked with great force until I was aware of all of my particles having been pressed into something very small, very dense, and very heavy.

And then just as suddenly as everything had begun, the motion stopped with a horrible sound and feeling---

Wham!!

I crash landed back into my physical body.

And it hurt. Bigtime.

It felt like I had slammed into a brick wall and at the same time I had *become* the thing I had hit. I certainly felt as dense as a brick wall when I first returned from heaven.

Existing in a bodiless state was perfection. Being crammed back into a body was like being in an overly small prison cell made of brick walls --and my own body constituted the bricks of my imprisonment.

I remember thinking: No wonder babies cry when they are born.

Chapter 21

Back in a Body

I have no recollection of being put into a wheelchair, but my memories pick back up when I was sitting in one. I was still very heavily medicated. I was aware that I had just returned from heaven, and I knew who I was and what my surgery had been for. I was generally unaware of and uninterested in my surroundings beyond the wheelchair, and I do not even know if a man or woman was pushing me.

My dear girlfriend, Marianna, was the only person I had told about the details of my operation beforehand. She had driven me to the surgery site and was there in the waiting room when I was brought out afterwards. I recognized her by her voice and heard her voice asking someone (perhaps the person pushing my wheelchair?) why I had been gone so much longer than was normal for this procedure.

What I perceived as a floating voice responded to her question: "We had a harder time than expected getting her to come out from under the anesthesia."

These words found their way into my ears and then clunked into my brain like coins thunking into a vending machine, falling in one by one. It took some time for the individual items going in to be sorted and tallied.

CLUNK.

I had been gone too long.   PAUSE. PAUSE. PAUSE.

CLUNK.

The unknown voice indicated I had had a problem with the anesthesia. The voice said nothing more.

My brain, which had been so alert when I'd been **out** of my body such a short time ago, was now no longer alert at all. In fact, it now seemed to be working in a disjointed manner and in exasperatingly slow motion. I waited for the individual words to arrange themselves into some further meaning while feeling oddly disconnected from this processing taking place within me.

TALLY..... TALLY...... TALLY.....

Brain: They aren't going to let on about what just happened. They are not going to say anything about the fact that I died in that room.

Soul: It's fine. That's about them, not about us/Leslie. They may be afraid of a lawsuit. There's a lot of fear in this dimension. Besides, they have no idea what **really** just happened. What they say or don't say has no impact on what we now know.

For the first time in my life, I was acutely aware of my brain and my soul having very different perspectives, and therefore, different agendas. The brain was trying to make sense of it all and "make things right" in an earthly context while my soul looked at the situation from a much higher vantage point and saw that earthly battles of this sort are completely unnecessary.

I seemed to be observing even this inner conversation from a distance. And then, the tally now evidently complete, something shifted inside me and the vending machine of self gave its offering.

There is no need to talk with anyone here about what happened.

ISSUE DROPPED.

I faded out and the next thing I remember was a searing pain that blinded me to all *except* the pain shooting through my torso.

Someone is trying to move this body. The floating voice is back... Saying it is time to go.

166

Brain: I am not at ALL ready to move or be moved. Moving hurts!! What's wrong with the people who work here? ... Making me leave when I still can't even move my body on my own?!!? Grrrrrrrr!

Soul: We're back on earth now. Yes. There **is** a lot of pain in this body... our/my/Leslie's body! I wonder how I am going to get into that car with all this pain. Let's focus on something wonderful instead of the pain. Marianna is so wonderful to help me this way. I love her so. What a dear friend.

I noted mutely that I had no control whatsoever over the muscles of this body, my body. I felt like a rag doll with pain sensors. Slow and floppy... and in a lot of pain, I observed that Sweet Marianna was having a very hard time maneuvering me into her car because I was unable to help her with even the smallest things as she attempted to move me. My feet were not responding to my brain's commands to move. My arms would not stay around Marianna's neck but instead slid off-- and I merely watched them slide as if they were not my arms but the arms of a person whose body I just happened to be looking out from.

She had made several attempts to get me into the car when a male voice came toward the car. The person that the voice was coming from assisted Marianna in getting me into the car, and then that same person got into the car with us. Marianna started to drive, and I winced in pain as the car moved.

I begged her to go much more slowly than she was, and she told me she was only backing out of the parking spot! When we got out onto the road, I heard myself moaning as we went over what felt like continual railroad tracks. Marianna assured me she was driving on the smoothest possible roads at the slowest possible speed.

I felt myself drifting in and out of consciousness in the car, and then Marianna gently shook me to let me know we were now at my home. Marianna, aided by the mystery male, somehow carried floppy Leslie to the couch and then stayed with me for the first 24 hours-- until my mind was clear and I was mentally back.

However, after the medication was out of my system, I found myself dealing with other issues. Even though I was accepting of the idea of being back in a body, that body now hurt even more than it had the day before. I could not move at all without feeling as if I was being stabbed, yet my mind was fully functional. This was a bad combination considering the timing of things because it meant I had a lot of time to sit and do nothing except think... and all I could think about was heaven and the differences between there and where I now was. My brain took over and my soul stepped back, and these comparisons that started on the couch went on for months.

Of course, I had known for a long time before my surgery that the human body is made of solids and liquids, and I had been aware that it's a basic tenet of physics that the vibrational level of things in the form of liquids and solids is denser than the vibrational level of gases – and consciousness and light. Yet I hadn't considered what the consequences of those facts would be when I'd been in heaven and had agreed to come back to earth. If I *had* thought of them and had had any idea how difficult this transition back to denser states would be, I am not sure I would have had the courage to return.

I was now all too aware that in order to exist, to physically **BE,** in a form on earth, the level of vibration must be much different than that of heaven. To be in bodies on earth, we necessarily need a slower and lower vibration than we have in heaven. We couldn't be in a physical form otherwise. Our bodies are mostly liquid with some solid components, and this is simply part of the way things are configured in this dimension. Having a slow, low vibration is a part of life in a body on planet earth.

UGH!!!

In heaven there are no slow, low vibrations. Nothing in heaven is in a solid or liquid state. Everything there is consciousness and light and even the "densest" beings I met were my heaven team members—who CHOSE to condense temporarily into denser formations only so that I would recognize them.

This extreme contrast between the vibrational state in heaven and that of being in a body on earth was hard to acclimate to. The vibrational situation on earth bothered me in the way an itchy sweater does. It's uncomfortable and you want to get out of it. I wanted out of my body. There were several reasons for this.

Since the particles are a LOT closer together in the liquid and solid states than in the heaven state, and since in liquids and solids the particles also move slower—much slower than in gases and much, **much** slower than light—being back in a body felt heavy and slow. I felt I was overly dense and that all of my particles were now moving and vibrating much more slowly than I wanted. Additionally, everything and everyone around me also seemed to be vibrating in slow motion. For these reasons, the energy of my own being and that of those around was not easy for me to be near.

This issue of density was compounded by the lack of freedom created by being in a body itself. I no longer felt that I *was* my body, yet unlike an itchy sweater than can be taken off quite easily, I could not get **out** of my body. I felt I was stuck "wearing" this body that had a dense/slow state.

Additionally, since in heaven I existed as pure consciousness, and since my consciousness traveled at the speed of light and the particles of my essence separated and reunited with itself/themselves and intermingled with others and absorbed knowledge and light and did *all sorts* of other spectacular things-- all without having to take a body along, this whole "having to take a body everywhere I want to go" aspect of earth was literally, a huge drag.

I felt as if my body was just a thing that I had to lug with me everywhere. It was almost as if my body was like a very big and bulky bag of potatoes. While I had accepted that I was going to be in a body for the duration of my time on earth, I still didn't feel integrated into my body-- not in the least.

On top of all that, having a body not only meant I had to *move* the body, but I was also shackled with needing to bathe the body, feed the body, clothe the body, rest the body, and an endless list of other things that were necessary to keep the body going. All this body stuff seemed an insane waste of energy!

Of course, I could not merely "think" my way to a new position in an instant now either. Instead of just **being** where I wanted to be in the moment I desired it, I now had to pass through time -and experience the space along the way- in order to get to where I was going, and *that* seemed a poor use of time and energy as well since I now knew it is not necessary to travel this way.

When I had been on earth with no knowledge of any other sort of existence, the moving-through-space-in-time-in-a-body part of earth had seemed normal. But upon getting back into that body and carrying with me knowledge and experience of a different way of being and moving, I struggled mightily to accept my physicality back on earth and longed to be back in heaven.

In general, my brain's perspective and agenda were what I saw and listened to when I first got back. I focused on the things that earth is not, and in doing this I forgot about what I'd learned. Instead, I only thought of where I wasn't: heaven.

Because of this, I initially felt like I had made a huge mistake in deciding to come back to earth. Rather than appreciating all that had happened to me and being thankful for my life, I instead primarily just longed to be back in the light. There were more than a few times when the feeling of being homesick for heaven was so strong that I broke down and all-out wept for heaven.

My vibration had been so extremely high while in heaven and now it was so much lower that the difference in these two states felt painful to me. Also, because my vibration was somewhat low -even for a person on earth- due to my continued thoughts about where I wasn't and what I didn't have the ability to do on earth, that I did not initially have access to a lot of the messages I had been given in heaven.

I was a certified open water scuba diver before my trip to heaven, and so I knew that divers in training all learn about the dangers of fast, massive changes in pressure. When divers go down into a body of water, the pressure increases the further down they go. Coming back up to the surface too rapidly after being at depth underwater-- where the pressure is so much greater than on the surface of the earth-- can have dire consequences.

If divers ascend from the depths too quickly, the rapid change in pressure can result in physical problems including bubbles forming in the blood. This is so painful that divers with this typically bend over from the horrible pain—in what has come to be known informally as *the bends*. It is more formally known as decompression sickness because of the fact that it

173

occurs when the pressure on/in the body decompresses too quickly—as in a fast diving ascent.

It is not the change in pressure alone that is problematic in these cases. It is the **speed** *in relationship to these large changes in pressure* that can be harmful. Hence, all trained divers know that a rapid pressure change (fast ascent) should be avoided whenever possible.

If a diver **does** ascend too rapidly, a hyperbaric (recompression) chamber may be used to help with decompression sickness. These chambers work by simulating the high pressure environment of being underwater, and then they slowly bring the pressure back to atmospheric levels. In this way, recompression chambers can offer a diver suffering from decompression sickness the opportunity to acclimate to pressure changes at a slower rate. This can often resolve medical issues resulting from this type of fast pressure change.

While divers go from high pressure to low pressure as they ascend, I had done the reverse: I had taken an extremely fast *downward* dive: I had gone from the very low pressure situation in heaven to the high pressure environment on the surface of the earth, and I had done it very quickly. In other words, I experienced a rapid *descent* when I came back from heaven to earth. And I felt as if I had a form of *re*compression sickness as a result.

I longed for a decompression chamber to help me move more slowly from being decompressed to compressed... so that I could take more time and gradually acclimate to being back on earth.

I was unable to access such a chamber.

Chapter 22

The Body Irony

I had my near death experience after I had decided I wanted to go under the knife to physically enhance my breasts. In other words, I underwent **elective** surgery for breast augmentation. Nothing was medically wrong with my breasts. This was a *purely cosmetic* operation. I was so concerned about my body's shape that I paid money to have it surgically altered. Yet due to the events that happened in that very surgery, when I came out of the surgery, I had no interest in my physical body apart from its use for carrying my soul from place to physical place while back here on earth.

Let me be clear. In the days immediately after my surgery, I didn't want to be on earth *at all*. I didn't want anything to do with *anything* in this physical realm, I certainly didn't want a dense physical body that I'd need to drag around in order to go wherever my soul wanted to go, and I couldn't have cared less about the shape of my breasts.

My perspective changed with time as I adjusted to being back in a physical form, but the initial shock of being in a dense form after having been without any physical form whatsoever was hard to bear. I felt that everything on earth was heavy and irritatingly dense. Everything looked *not delicate* and *not perfect* when compared to the delicate perfection of heaven.

I finally had what I'd been dreaming of for years: beautiful breasts that were proportionate with my height and weight. But because of what I experienced during the surgery, I suddenly had very little interest in my physical body-- and the shape of my breasts was the last thing on my mind.

So, the surgery to give me the body I had dreamed of resulted in me not focusing on my physicality. Little by little I learned to laugh at this... and I realized there was probably a message from heaven in this situation...somewhere. And indeed there was. It was linked to communication which was also extremely frustrating for me when I first returned to my body.

Chapter 23

Language Frustrations_

In addition to my back-in–a-body frustrations, I also dealt with language frustrations upon my return. When I first came back to earth, being back in a realm where communication via light is *not* the norm was not easy for me. I did not want to go back to communicating the way I had done prior to my trip to heaven.

Of course, on the one hand, it makes perfect sense that in a physical world, communication is a physical thing. On earth we are in physical bodies and are in a physical dimension where we have all the physical, linguistic-related conditions needed to precisely make and manipulate sound. We also have everything we need to process these vibrations and decode their assigned meanings.

This mode of communication is a match in many ways for this physical realm, and earth's languages have important roles here in this realm of separation. But when I first returned from heaven, all I saw were weaknesses in earth languages. Rooted primarily in separation, these aspects of earth languages were almost unbearable for me initially.

Separation within languages on earth begins at the level of the words themselves. Words are separate from the things they signify. There is the thing, and then there is the word which represents that thing. When we communicate via earth languages, we necessarily use the words that represent the things we want to discuss rather than using the things themselves. Every earth language, in this regard, is indirect. From the foundation, earth languages start with separation between the actual thing and the word which represents that thing.

Beyond that, because different groups have assigned different specific meanings to different given sounds, different languages have come to exist on earth. Within languages, there are often different dialects as well, furthering separation.

When we communicate with earth languages, there is also always a chance that we might be misunderstood because we never know exactly how another will interpret what we are attempting to communicate. All sorts of things can get in the way. The ultimate reason for miscommunication among fluent speakers of the same earth language who are attempting to communicate sincerely is separate perspectives: we simply cannot be sure of the perspective from which another is sending a message when we use earth languages.

If someone dear to you says they love the color blue, what exactly does that mean to you? What does it mean to the person who said it? Are they the same?

Can you ever be certain?

With an earth language, the answer to that last question is always going to be an emphatic NO. We cannot be certain we ever understand exactly what another means when we communicate with earth languages. We may have a general concept of a speaker's intended meaning--especially if both parties are fluent in the earth language being spoken-- but we cannot possibly know <u>exactly</u> what another means when we communicate with earth languages.

Our separate eyes and brains may process the information differently. When we look out at the world and see it, we never know if others see things exactly the same way. Maybe what I see as blue is different from what you see as blue.

Then there are connotations. All of the things you have experienced in your life have given you individualized connotations related to different words. Blue may have connotations of "baby boy" for one person, while for another it may be associated with the ocean (and all of the positive or negative experiences of that person related to the ocean). Perhaps it is the color of a person's alma mater or maybe it reminds you of that perfect vacation sky. The list could go on indefinitely, and so a chance for misunderstanding is certainly present even if we are discussing things that are visible—like colors. Intangibles are even less easy to convey well in earth languages.

For all of these reasons, miscommunications within earth languages can occur even when people intend to communicate sincerely. Of course, not all people enter into earthly communication with integrity. Individuals may choose to stretch the truth or even outright lie in earth languages.

These conditions result in earth languages being indirect, imprecise, and in many ways quite ineffective. This had never bothered me before my trip to heaven because at that time I knew of no other way of communicating. But now? Now I knew about a completely different form of communication, and with this other form of communication, none of these issues exist. I longed to be able to use that purer form of communication here on earth.

Heaven communicates in a form of language that does not need a physical dimension for its existence and in which there is no possibility of miscommunication. This stems from the fact that language in heaven uses the actual essence of things for communication. What is being sent outward IS the thing that is being communicated. While on earth words represent things but are not the things themselves, in heaven the things **themselves** are shared directly. In other words, it is the thing *itself*, existing in the form of energy, which is exchanged during communication in something like a transfer. I said earlier that heaven does not use "words" in the way we understand words to exist on earth, and this is what I meant by that.

These messages are relayed in light which is love, and because love is the fabric of all, this is how it is possible to actually energetically send the essence of the message AS the message via a form of love/light "telepathy".

Misunderstanding is not even an option with this form of communication! Because the message is the essence of the thing itself and not a marker to represent the thing, the foundation of communication in heaven starts with unity.

Miscommunication from a lack of understanding the other's perspective is not an option in heaven either--by virtue of the fact that there is really only one perspective in heaven, and that is the perspective of pure love.

Another way that language in heaven is really different from language on earth is that the communication in heaven is occurring between parts of a larger, interconnected system.

Further, this larger system, the whole, contains knowledge of all.

I was connected to the information "bank" belonging to the larger whole in such a way that I had access to anything I wanted to know. This meant that even when I didn't know something myself, I could get the answer from what was essentially just a different part of my larger self. I did not need to leave the system of "larger self" in order to communicate: I was merely communicating with a different aspect of myself when I asked questions and got answers. This is not the case on earth and this is due, again, to the nature of separation here.

As a side note, the access I had to all of this knowledge was in itself quite an interesting concept. It has some similarities to being connected to the internet. While connected to the internet, you are able to look up answers to anything you are interested in knowing about. While you don't *directly* know everything that is out there on the internet, through your connection to the internet you have access to all of the knowledge on the internet. The way I had access to all the knowledge of heaven was somewhat similar.

With the Internet, however, things aren't *exactly* as they are in heaven. Once we find the information we are looking for on the internet, we still need to read it and process it. In heaven the accessed knowledge is instantaneously understood. Upon asking, there is simply a knowing. Each time I thought of a question, the answer was mine immediately and completely. Plus, even when we are connected to the internet, we do not usually feel we ARE the internet. Again, there is separation in the earth dimension.

Through heaven's way of communicating, I came to understand everything I have ever wanted to know about anything at all. I posed questions and as fast as I could think of them I knew the answers. What is life? Who am I? Where am I now? Am I dead? What really happened to the dinosaurs? Why is life so painful? What is cancer? Is the earth going to end soon? Why do children die? Why am I here now?

It is precisely because the essences themselves *are* the messages that there is no need to mentally process a thing. Because receiving a message and understanding a message are one and the same, I was able to understand things in heaven that I could never have comprehended upon earth. Anything related to the history of the universe, mathematics, physics, space, GOD... all of it. I knew it all, and I myself was actually a *part* of the knowledge of it all as well.

Through the language of heaven, I grasped everything perfectly and immediately. This was all possible because

184

everything in heaven is love and the communication itself is love as well.

Receiving communication in essence form from the essences of others and sending messages in this same way out from my own essence to others was one of the grandest joys I experienced in heaven. This method of communication seemed perfect, like everything else in heaven.

When I got back to earth, with what I now knew about a more direct method of communication, using earth languages seemed like going from communicating with the latest high-tech phone to communicating only with smoke signals. It was extremely frustrating.

It also seemed unnecessary. Now that I knew there was/is a better way to communicate, I longed to use that and to stop using earth languages altogether.

At this point I was still very much in my head. Whenever I thought about heaven, which was nearly all the time, I wanted to share the wonders of heaven with the people I love on earth, but it seemed **unbearable** to be left with only the option of explaining heaven via a language of earth—for I knew I would not be able to do heaven justice in explaining it in an earth language.

Instead, I longed to share about heaven using my soul and light/love. I wanted to communicate about the realm of light while using the language of that realm, but I had no idea how to do that.

Another language frustration quickly arose for me. It was related to my work. Before my visit to heaven, I had spent my entire professional life working with language...earth language. Previously, all of the languages of earth had simply fascinated me, I had loved my work, and my work had seemed a perfect fit for me. Now, I no longer had the same love for my work because of my language frustrations. The one area of my life that had been firmly anchored for my entire adult life was now unmoored.

I was adrift in my work life...and in my earth life in general. I knew I had come back to earth for a reason, but I had no idea whatsoever what it was. I felt like the answers were somewhere nearby, but I didn't know how to find them. I wanted out of my body and out of this place where people spoke in smoke signals. My mind was cluttered and I was completely in my head about all of it. Being back on earth felt almost too much to bear. It was a dark time for me.

Chapter 24

The Trees Talk to Me

While I did not feel good (understatement!!) when I first returned, I did slowly find ways to feel better. One way was to spend time in nature. Another way was running.

I got the idea to start running because I had run on and off my entire life, and it had always lifted my spirits and reconnected me with my inner self. I had also always run *outside* so that was a natural choice for me. I found that when I combined the two, I felt lighter and more comfortable on earth.

When I ran outside, it now felt different than it had previously. From as early as my first days back, I had noticed that being outside was a different experience for me than it had ever been previously. Even if there was only a single tree near me, I somehow FELT the tree without touching it. I was far more attuned to nature, and I felt a completely different relationship to nature than I had ever felt before. This was a big change because prior to my trip to heaven, I had never felt any real connection to nature at all, and this profound change in me was one of the first of the many spiritual changes I noted upon my return.

Even in my low (compared to heaven) vibrational state, I still carried within me the knowledge of the things I had learned in the realm of light. However, while the journey to heaven itself was with me in vivid detail, the knowledge I had gained there seemed to be inside me in a kind of sleeping state. Yet it was as if these truths were resonating within me at the cellular level because even though I wasn't aware of them consciously, they somehow guided me to run outside.

Once I was running outside, it was the trees that initially helped me consciously remember the first pieces of the knowledge I had gained in heaven. They did this by helping me raise my frequency and also through reminding me that we are all one. Their communication method was/is very similar to the way that information is communicated in heaven, and they themselves are very close to heaven.

As we know, all of the particles in heaven are shimmering... vibrating. All of them. All the time. The frequency of the shimmering in heaven is so high and light that it may be hard for us to even imagine from here on earth-- where our human frequencies are generally much lower and denser. However, the plants on earth generally vibrate at a frequency closer to heaven than most humans, and the plants on the planet are sending out a very pure, clear love. Because they are closer to their essence while on earth than most humans, it is easier for them to send this pure love consistently.

Today I love the trees, all trees, dearly. However, I am especially fond of one tree in particular: a bushy, somewhat lopsided tree along the street where I regularly run. This was the first tree that I understood as it spoke with me early one morning just after I had finished running.

As I stood beneath the tree, I felt the tree's love for me. I felt the tree sending me love. ….And I sent love back to the tree, just as I had sent love back to GODLIGHT in heaven.

In that instant, I understood that I was the tree and the tree was me and we are both a part of the all, and so we are both little pieces of God and are, therefore, both beautiful and sacred. This knowing seemed so simple and clear that I couldn't believe I hadn't noticed it previously.

The poem below captures what I felt as I stood beneath "my" tree on that very special morning.

Beautiful, blessed, sacred tree

Gently shining down on me.

Standing in your love I see--

Beautiful, blessed, sacred me.

189

I suddenly remembered that although while on earth we are in separate forms, these forms are not our true essence—not for any of us in any form. For each of us, our true essence is that part of us that comes out of the body when the physical body dies. It is the part of us that went into the body when the body came to life, and it is the part of us that lives beyond the body of the earth dimension. This is true for every human. It is also true for every tree and flower, every bird and butterfly.

I felt almost like I was in a movie with staging when a yellow butterfly went by just as the word butterfly entered my thoughts. The butterfly seemed to smile at me.

Then a fully formed love-filled knowing was suddenly in my thoughts, and I softly and lovingly whispered the following to the butterfly:

Beautiful butterfly, I see you flutter by.

I know that I am you, and you are me.

Now I was *sure* that the butterfly was smiling at me, and I also felt my tree telling me that these words had come to me in a message from my heaven team. I was sure that was true. One of them had definitely whispered both of these poems to me. Had it been Whitman? I felt it likely had.

The more I was outside after I began to listen to the trees, the more messages and love I received from them, and it was in this way that the trees initially helped me lift my vibration. The trees are our friends and it is no mistake, no chance or random thing, that the trees give us oxygen and we give them carbon dioxide. We are partners in this earth realm. As our partners, they want to give us much more than merely oxygen. They love to give us love.

Today on earth, I feel a connection to nature that is nothing short of holy. The connection I feel with nature is very much like what I learned about and experienced in heaven when I was mingled in with the "all" of heaven. When we can remember our larger, interconnected whole while in separate forms on earth, everything on earth feels different.

Yes. You are you, and I am me. Certainly that is true. But we also comprise a larger WE, and this is true for all entities in nature.

I am sure that all of nature is communicating with all of us all the time. In order to hear it, a good place to start is spending time out in nature while sending nature love. This will raise our frequency. Over time, we can become close enough to the frequency of the communication form the trees are using to be able to hear them.

Because the trees are communicating with light and they are very close to the frequency of heaven, to get nearer to their frequency, we need to get "lighter", become more light-filled. Of course, we do this by flowing more love.

As I ran more and spent more time in nature sending love outward to the trees and also absorbing the love and messages from the trees, I was starting to feel lighter and more comfortable in my body.

Chapter 25

Reconnection to Heaven

Another day when I was running, I was listening to the trees as I had by then been doing for quite some time. The trees had told me running was good for my soul and would help me adjust to being back on earth, so I was running a lot. On this particular day, I felt them giving me some kind of a message about breathing... and something about them telling me *that* reminded me of the importance of breathing to the universe. All the knowledge and messages from GODLIGHT about breathing returned in a flash.

I began to focus on my breathing and found that when I did this, it kept me in the present moment and it also lifted me up vibrationally.

And then, as I breathed, I spontaneously began to appreciate the beauty I saw and felt around me: the trees, their messages, GODLIGHT.

As I appreciated, I remembered more about light! Another huge package of information was suddenly "known" to me. All of the information about flowing love that GODLIGHT had given me opened as if I had just somehow typed in the correct secret password.

I knew all GODLIGHT had told me about flowing and giving love and how we can send light this way on earth if we choose... and I was so joyful I felt I might float away with happiness.

I was joyful about having the knowledge but also because it was like I was back in GODLIGHT's arms! His words were there again in all of their original clarity and with all of the original love that the messages had been transmitted in. I felt *so much love*. It WAS heavenly. Tears of joy ran down my cheeks as I ran underneath my beloved friends, the trees.

I sent love to GODLIGHT just as I had done in heaven except this time, I was in a body. I felt the light go out from my heart and I knew I was sending love back to GODLIGHT from my location on earth in a body. In that moment, I loved my body because I understood that it carries my soul and that my body allows me to send love while on earth.

After sending love to GODLIGHT for some time, I felt lighter than I ever had since returning to earth. It was wonderful! Then I had the idea (or more likely GODLIGHT or the trees or a member of my heaven team *gave* me the idea) to send love out to the people I passed and who passed me as I ran. I was running on the sidewalk of a busy South Florida road. The oncoming traffic was such that a car was zooming past me every few seconds. Sometimes groups of cars would approach me and speed by. I had never previously paid any attention to the cars on the streets when I ran.

Now, I looked at a car and pushed light out from my heart to the car. I literally sent light to the car and the driver in the car. It felt amazing to do this! I picked another car and did the same thing to that car and *its* passengers.

All this time, I was continuing to run and without even trying, I felt my pace increasing. My breathing was steady and strong and I was in the zone where I knew I could keep this pace for hours if I wanted to.

The way love was pouring from me was incredible. I was giving love to people who would never know what I was doing. The anonymity of pure giving in this way was thrilling. I was wrapping them in love the way that GODLIGHT had wrapped me in love in heaven. I noticed that as I did this, I felt lighter and lighter and lighter until I giggled wondering if my feet might actually leave the earth soon-- that I might just float away because I was so light-filled and vibrationally high.

The royal palm trees that lined the road along this section of my path were now an orchestra blasting out something that I later learned was Beethoven's *Ode to Joy*.

Everything around me was humming in tune. The birds, the flowers, the wind... all of them seemed to be sending me messages from heaven. All of them were thrilled that I had remembered the way to communicate in heaven while on earth.

It was SO spectacularly fun! I felt like Cinderella must have felt when her fairy godmother granted her her wish. I was back in heaven, and I was also on earth! I was one with all on earth and ALL in heaven, and it was the closest I could imagine being to heaven while on earth.

I sent love to every car that came toward me and then began sending light to groups of cars. Soon I was sending light to all the buildings and all the people *in* all the buildings I passed. Then I added in the trees, the ground, the sky, the air itself... I was blanketing all with light and love.

I was BREATHING love and light to everyone and everything that was anywhere in my vicinity. I felt myself glowing with the love of heaven and I felt radiant.

While I was doing this, I was on earth, but I felt like I was in heaven again!! I felt GODLIGHT there with me as I ran. The trees were angels sending me their love and I felt GODLIGHT sending me love as well.

It WAS indeed exactly as GODLIGHT had promised. I would never feel alone again. I am part of the ALL and now I knew I would be able to talk with anyone on my Heaven Team at any time if I only breathed and lived with light as GODLIGHT had told me I would do.

Now I remembered what he had said. Now the knowledge was easily accessible.

I finished my 2.5-mile loop and decided to repeat the loop to do another 2.5 miles. I was suddenly stronger and more powerful than I had ever known myself to be.

I continued running and was now blanketing the entire city I was in with light. Then I sent out love to the entire Fort Lauderdale metropolitan area and every person, animal and plant within it.

The more I did this, the lighter I felt. I was not only now feeling better than since returning from heaven, I now felt better than I had EVER felt while on earth.

When the entire region I was in was filled with light, I went on to send light to all of Florida, all of the country, all of the planet and out beyond up to heaven-- my True Home, the beloved Realm of Light.

Chapter 26

At Peace

Now it all made sense. Everything related to my body and communication had been so frustrating for me after my return because I had been given a message in heaven that I was supposed to be doing something *different* with my body and language than I had done with them before my visit to heaven. Until I actually started to do those new and different things, I could not feel at home on earth with my body or with communication.

But that first day that I ran and sent love to all, I knew I was communicating in the purest and truest language of all and I knew that the body was the transceiver, the transponder, the amplifier: the perfect vessel for sending this type of heavenly communication while on earth.

I now understood/saw/knew/felt the fuller picture. I saw it all from a higher perspective...from heaven's perspective. Only with a body are we able to send love and light this way while on earth.

Now, rather than feeling that being in a body is like an itchy, uncomfortable sweater, I see that a body is the PERFECT form for this dimension. It can receive, focus, and then resend the light from heaven outward.

Our bodies are sacred because they are a part of the ALL and they carry our souls while on earth, but our bodies are also spectacular tools that allow us to communicate on earth as is done in heaven-- and even to communicate with heaven itself while on earth.

I had been aching to communicate this way ever since my return without realizing exactly what I had been yearning for. Now I saw it clearly: my body itself IS the tool that allows me to communicate as in heaven while on earth.

I felt a new appreciation for and acceptance of my body, but I also felt a deep love and respect for my body in a way that I had not previously.

Since that time I have been working with light on earth in wonderful and beautiful ways. By working with light and making "light choices" each of us can raise our vibration, and when we raise our vibration, many amazing things happen.

Remember that butterfly that showed up at the perfect moment? Things like that happen to me ALL THE TIME now. As we flow light, we ourselves become lighter (more full of light) and lighter (vibrationally less dense). The more I work with light -- sending it to everyone and everything that I encounter -- the more light-filled I become. As I fill with light, I am lighter in all senses of the word. When I am lighter, my vibration is also closer to heaven while here on earth, and heavenly things happen as the norm!

There is a new-found peace within me. All is one and all is well. I *know* this now. When I get a lot of light moving through me rapidly, I feel myself getting lighter until I reach a point where I hear those in heaven begin to speak to me. Of course, they have been speaking to me (and all of us) all along, but it is only when I am in a "high" enough place myself, that I begin to hear their messages.

All in nature on earth and all on my heaven team up in heaven know my name, and they are my dear friends. Though I know all of nature is calling to me, at this point I generally only hear the largest trees. I get the sense that this is because (due to their size) their messages are amplified. I am sure that in time, as I continue to work even more with light, I will hear even more of nature speaking to me. I am at peace about this as well.

Chapter 27

The Secret of Love

Love is a language. It is not a new language at all. It is the oldest language, the original language, the essence of communication. It is the language of heaven and it is also the language of all of nature here on earth. Additionally, it is the true first language for each of us humans here on earth. Since we all come here from heaven, we all *already* know this language when we arrive on earth.

Anyone who has spent time with a newborn knows this to be true. When a baby is first born, the baby *speaks* to its family in love long before being able to speak in any human language.

And love is the same beautiful language that a parent uses when holding a child. When two best girlfriends in high school look at each other across a classroom and then giggle about something only they understand, they are using the language of love. Lovers use this language when they look in each other's eyes or touch one another. It is even the language my friend in the perfume booth in Egypt used to talk with his beloved perfumes.

Communication in love involves consciously choosing to flow a loving message outward from our heart region toward another. We can direct this light/love toward any item or person we choose, and then we can "beam" it to them. It is like a beautiful secret message... and it is powerful for both the sender and the receiver. Anyone can choose to communicate with anyone else on earth or elsewhere in this way. Anyone can choose to send light to one and all.

The more of this light/love we give, the more light-filled we become, and the more we will see everything in our lives lifted to a higher place. The resulting higher frequency of our own bodies allows us to be able to speak with nature and heaven --which is spectacular.

But EVERY aspect of our lives will be lighter. When we live this way, sending light to one and all, we are healthy, we are joyful, our relationships are beautiful, we see amazing "coincidences" all around us, and we have material wealth as well if that is our desire.

If we flow love and choose a life of light, life feels like heaven on earth. This is so because when we live this way, we are BEing heavenly while on earth, and in doing so (among many other wonderful benefits) we rise above our problems. We no longer need to depend on the helicopter pilot for a better view; we are able to fly ourselves and can see the better choices for ourselves.

We can opt use this language every day, in every moment. And if we choose to communicate with love on earth in all of our communications, we will find our lives transformed. Speaking in love, the language of heaven, is a choice we can each make at any moment. It is never too late to use our true first language here on earth by following light. What I speak of here is the language of love and those who speak it have a portal to heaven while on earth. This portal to heaven on earth is the secret of giving love.

Chapter 28

New Life

Living these truths has created beautiful results. Life is joyful. I feel like I have become a fountain overflowing with love. I am now happy with myself and with my life in a way I never imagined was possible before. Feeling wonderful is now normal for me, and this new normal is a wonderful way to live.

I still have days when I wake up feeling a bit grumpy, things still go wrong in my life from time to time, and life is not entirely perfect... but the roller coaster days are gone. And when something *does* go wrong, I respond from a different place now.

Since I know this is not the ultimate reality, it's easier to be objective about things. I find I am more neutral than I ever was before, and I realize that whatever is going wrong is a result of my own choices. I have no one to blame now except myself when things don't go as I'd like, and so if I get a result I didn't want, I think back to what I've been "giving" recently. Generally, if things aren't going as I'd like in any area of my life, I can trace it back to me not flowing enough love to that area of my life or to me not allowing more love to flow in when I *do* send out love. This review process helps me to refocus and move forward.

I find that "normal" now is at a really high place and that I can indeed find sufficient variety in switching from one wonderful thing to another—such that there is no need to keep life interesting through the drama created from really low lows.

There is also a peace within me that is solid because of all I now know and because of the fact that anytime I want to know something else, I know I can just ask-- and someone from my heaven team will give me the answer.

Although there is still darkness in the earth dimension, I am no longer afraid of it in the way I was before. In fact, I have realized that most of the things we are afraid of stem from a fear of death. Now that I am no longer afraid of death because of my knowing that death does not even exist in the way I always imagined it did, I find fear holds little power over me. When I do feel fear about something, I shine light on it and examine what it is that I am afraid of and then take action from a place of love. Generally, I try to remember GODLIGHT's message that anything that does not feel like love is a false truth.

Another freeing aspect of my new life is the lack of concern about how others view me. I know who I am, and I am fine with whatever others think of me. While it never feels great to be ridiculed or insulted, words meant to hurt no longer pierce my heart in the way they used to. I know GODLIGHT loves me through and through and through and through, and I love myself that much as well. When others see me in a way that is not filled with love, I understand that that is about *them* and where they are in their own journey. My choice to send them love in that moment is about where I am in my journey.

Of course, this new way of living only began *after* that difficult initial period of adjustment after my surgery. And, speaking of the surgery, to this day I don't know-- and I am not the least bit interested in knowing—what happened to me medically that day. I never asked because after the whole thing was over, the medical explanation was irrelevant to me. I know what I experienced and how it changed me and the way I live on earth, and that is really all I have ever cared about. I regularly send light from afar to the doctor who performed my surgery, and I have even referred friends to him. He is a fine doctor. My trip to heaven was not about him as much as it was about me.

Flowing love has lifted my vibration, and I now live in the moment and send love in the moment. I appreciate my way through the day sending love to myself, to all in my vicinity, all around the planet, and up to my friends in heaven.

My Heaven Team talks with me regularly. I love them dearly and they are with me as I write these words—encouraging me, cheering me on, and reminding me that I can do anything I desire. (And so can YOU. Yes…. Y-O-U.)

I have learned to love myself which means I can also receive love from others now, and this has transformed all of my relationships. I am joyfully married to a wonderful man, and I also have the knowing that if I were ever to be a mother, I would be a wonderful one.

I am now writing which (as you know) has been a dream of mine for decades. Additionally, I have opened my own language school. Our focus at the moment is on earth languages, but I have just opened a conversation course in LIGHT in which we remind adults how to flow light/love in the language of heaven while on earth.

I am teeming with joy and my life is beautiful. I now know that I can, indeed, do anything. I am better than anyone else, but the truth is that we are *all* magnificent. We are all magnificent because we are all a part of the ALL. We are all pieces of God. We are all love in human form.

Oh! And the infamous abyss? It has not returned once since my visit to heaven.

Chapter 29

View from Above

So what did I learn while there? How would I sum up heaven's perspective if I was that pilot describing the view from above?

All along I had known that language is a portal that gives us different perspectives. It is why I loved language so dearly before my visit to heaven. What I learned in heaven, though, is that love/light is also a language. It is the language of heaven, and flowing love/light while here on earth opens a portal to heaven and to all that is in the Realm of Light.

In heaven I learned that I am loved – more than I ever imagined was possible, and that we are all loved this deeply.

I also learned that what we often see as tragedies or defects from the earth perspective are not that at all. They are part of a bigger plan that we cannot always see all of from earth.

From heaven's perspective, I have learned that there is no such thing as death and that we have free will in everything we choose including when to leave our bodies on earth. You will not leave earth until your soul is ready to go. No one does. When you leave your body, you continue to live and a new adventure awaits.

Heaven is filled with the essences of all: love, joy, light, truth, and all that is good and wonderful.

All that comes to earth is made of the love of heaven. Even if a being does not remember this truth, it remains a truth.

Heaven is made of love which in heaven is expressed as light. Light is conscious. It exists as particles of all, yet it also flows. It is both particle and flowing as surely as I am both a teacher and a sister-- even though at any given moment I may be expressing myself either as a teacher or a sister, but I am always both—and so light is always both particle and flowing.

For love to be "alive" it must flow. If we are not flowing love, we are not living life to the fullest. We can choose to flow love or not. This is part of free will.

Each time we make the most love-filled and love-flowing choice, we shift our vibration closer to the vibration of our essence, our heaven vibration, and this feels good because this is our true state. Each time we choose a less-loving, less-light, lower-vibration option, we move away from our essence and that feels less good.

I learned that we have a heaven team and that that person who is the biggest thorn in my/your foot may very well be a part of our heaven team acting out a pre-agreed-upon role in our life here on earth in order to give us the opportunity to flow love in every moment to every being on the planet—and especially to the people who are most difficult to love.

If we send love to everyone, everything changes. Not only does it raise our own frequency so that we literally go up higher and can transcend our problems. Beyond that, because we are all truly ONE, when we raise our own individual vibration, we raise the vibration of ALL.

Because of this, what you think and HOW you do the things you are doing really does make a difference.

If we follow our passions and live flowing love, we will find our soul's treasure chest on earth and this will show us what our soul's larger objective (beyond new experiences) was in coming to earth.

There is nothing to fear if we live in love. Fear is a false truth that does not exist in heaven. Love shifts fear to a higher vibration in the same way light shines into darkness and it is gone. These two (fear and darkness) are the same. One is the emotional aspect and the other is the visual aspect of a lack of love.

Love is all that exists. If we see other things than love, they are false truths that are merely appearing real in the way my abyss appeared very real to me for many years—yet it was only a false truth. If we flow love, false truths will fall away.

There is an unlimited supply of love in heaven. If we joyfully give all the love inside our souls, it will create a vacuum of love within us. Into this vacuum, if we invite it, love from heaven will flow so that we will never run out of love. We will always have more love to give because when we give joyfully, we will be refilled from heaven.

I learned that when we think a thought, in that instant it IS. This is true in heaven (immediately) and it is true on earth as well (although here there is a delay in its physical arrival).

I learned we are all our individual selves but we are also all part of the larger whole. To say that we are not connected to each other is like saying one part of the sky is not connected to another part of the sky. It is one sky. There are different clouds in the sky, but they are all a part of the sky, are they not? In the same way, we are all part of God. We are one.

I learned that love is an energy and we are all made from this energy, the energy of love.

Love cannot be held. It can only be flowed.

And because we are made of love and love must be given, we must give in order to fully live.

To give love is to flow it outwards from ourselves without any regard for whether or not it will ever return back to us, giving joyfully and completely the way water flows in the falls at Niagara. If we live this way, all of our cells will fill with light and our lives will be healthy in every way.

The key to living a happy, healthy, fulfilling life is to give love.

I learned that the closest we can get to heavenly communication while on earth is sending love/light.

Love is the fabric of all. Love is bigger than any problem and the ultimate answer to any problem is to send love to it. That is what the perspective from heaven ultimately allows us to see. It is all love: all of it. We are all love: all of us.

Love is the beginning, the essence, the answer to all of the questions.

Love is all.

ALL is love.

Chapter 30

Closing

It is a wonderful feeling to have this book transferred from my heart into words in an earth language. I have done my best to give you heaven's perspective through words. My heaven team is rejoicing for me because of the fact I have now finished this project. I feel their love flowing to me and know they are sending me love now—and always.

In particular, I feel Archangel Gabriel's joy that I have completed this book. He has told me many times that one reason I came back to earth was, in fact, to tell this story: to share what I experienced in heaven; to share these truths about light and love; to give people on earth an option for a different way of living.

This story, this way of living, is possible for everyone. These truths are available to any and all who ask to know of them.

I will be talking more about light and how to use it in heavenly ways in upcoming material, but for now, it is time to say good-bye.

Sending you the light that is love,
Leslie

Epilogue

GODLIGHT has a suggestion for a few last words here. He says he is pleased that I have remembered why I came back to earth. He also says the following:

The message of Heaven's Perspective is, in essence, LOVE.

This is because love IS all there really is. ALL that is IS love. We are all part of the ALL. We *are* love, and if we flow love to others joyfully, each part of the all --each of you, each of us-- can live as in heaven while on earth.

Made in the USA
Lexington, KY
31 January 2016